T0252059

Cyber Security Culture

Reviews for
Cyber Security Culture: Counteracting Cyber Threats through Organizational Learning and Training

This excellent book comes at a time when cyber security is paramount in the concerns of all organizations that handle information as an asset – that should be all of us. Relying on technical threat mitigation is not enough. What is required is a change of culture and this book is a first class exemplar of how to do this though changing the way we organize ourselves and how we train to address modern threats. It is a book for everyone with an interest in safeguarding their business and their organization.

Neil Fisher, Vice Chairman, Information Assurance
Advisory Council (www.iaac.org.uk)

Protecting critical information infrastructure will be a vital component of business, organisational and national security in the twenty-first century. Cyber threats – from hacking, terrorism, sabotage or espionage – are already widespread and on the increase, yet many organizations remain poorly prepared for dealing with such attacks. Trim and Upton's timely book takes a reasoned, well informed and practical approach to this complex topic, providing useful guidance to managers and emphasizing an organizational learning approach.

John Twigg, University College London, UK

This is a thoughtful and practical approach to handling cyber security incidents. Incident management is fast moving, requiring quick decision making which is directly dependent on knowledge and confidence. Building confidence through training and exercising is a valuable initiative.

Bruno Brunskill, Company Secretary, Information Assurance
Advisory Council (IAAC)

Cyber Security Culture

Counteracting Cyber Threats through Organizational Learning and Training

PETER TRIM
University of London

and

DAVID UPTON
Stirling Reid Ltd.

Routledge
Taylor & Francis Group

LONDON AND NEW YORK

First published 2013 by Gower Publishing

Published 2016 by Routledge
2 Park Square, Milton Park, Abingdon, Oxfordshire OX14 4RN
711 Third Avenue, New York, NY 10017, USA

First issued in paperback 2016

Routledge is an imprint of the Taylor & Francis Group, an informa business

Copyright © Peter Trim and David Upton 2013

Peter Trim and David Upton have asserted their moral right under the Copyright, Designs
and Patents Act, 1988, to be identified as the authors of this work.

Gower Applied Business Research
Our programme provides leaders, practitioners, scholars and researchers with thought
provoking, cutting edge books that combine conceptual insights, interdisciplinary rigour and
practical relevance in key areas of business and management.

Chapter's 1, 3, 4, 8, 9 © Peter Trim | Chapter's 2, 5, 7 © David Upton | Chapter 6 © Peter Trim
and David Upton

All rights reserved. No part of this book may be reprinted or reproduced or utilised in
any form or by any electronic, mechanical, or other means, now known or hereafter
invented, including photocopying and recording, or in any information storage or
retrieval system, without permission in writing from the publishers.

Notice:
Product or corporate names may be trademarks or registered trademarks, and are
used only for identification and explanation without intent to infringe.

British Library Cataloguing in Publication Data
Trim, Peter R. J.
  Cyber security culture : counteracting cyber threats
  through organizational learning and training.
  1. Cyberterrorism--Prevention--Management. 2. Business
  enterprises--Computer networks--Security measures.
  3. Employees--Training of.
  I. Title II. Upton, David.
  658.4'78-dc23

Library of Congress Cataloging-in-Publication Data
Trim, Peter R. J.
  Cyber security culture : counteracting cyber threats through organizational learning and
  training / by Peter Trim and David Upton.
     p. cm.
  Includes bibliographical references and index.
  ISBN 978-1-4094-5694-0 (hbk) 1. Information technology--Security measures.
  2. Computer security. 3. Computer crimes--Prevention. I. Upton, David. II. Title.
  HD30.2.T75 2013
  658.4'78--dc23

2012033279

ISBN 13: 978-1-138-27664-2 (pbk)
ISBN 13: 978-1-4094-5694-0 (hbk)

Contents

List of Figures

List of Tables

About the Authors

Peter Trim PhD is a Senior Lecturer in Management and Director of the Centre for Advanced Management and Interdisciplinary Studies (CAMIS) at Birkbeck College, University of London. He holds degrees from various institutions including City University, Cranfield Institute of Technology and Cambridge University. During his academic career he has taught a range of Marketing and Management courses in France, Hong Kong, the Netherlands and the UK. He has published widely in a number of areas including Strategic Marketing, Industrial Marketing, Management Education, Corporate Intelligence, Corporate Security and National Security; and was co-editor, with Jack Caravelli, of *Strategizing Resilience and Reducing Vulnerability*, which was published by Nova Science Publishers Inc. in 2009.

Dr Trim has worked in several industries and has participated in a number of academic, government and industry workshops, both in the UK and abroad. He is a member of a number of professional associations and was previously Chairman of the Society for the Advancement of Games and Simulations in Education and Training (SAGSET). He has also been involved in another research project under the Network Security – Information Infrastructure Protection programme, funded jointly by the Technology Strategy Board and SEEDA (South East England Development Agency).

David Upton is a Director of Stirling Reid Limited, a specialized consultancy company based in London, which has organized emergency response exercises in all continents and many industrial sectors. These have covered business continuity issues, industrial emergency response, and top-level crisis management. Stirling Reid Limited's clients include government organizations, agencies, utility companies, oil, gas, pharmaceutical, shipping and transportation companies. He is the author of various publications including 'Large emergency-response exercises: Qualitative characteristics – A survey' (Lee, Y.-I., Trim, P.R.J., Upton, J. and Upton, D. (2009). *Simulation & Gaming: An International Journal of Theory, Practice and Research*, 40 (6), 726–51).

David is a member of the National Council of the Society of Industrial Emergency Services officers (SIESO), the Emergency Planning Society, and the Institute of Energy. A graduate of Cambridge University, he also studied at London Business School. He was formerly in the British Diplomatic Service, where he served in British Embassies in South Africa, Iran and Australia, and was also a Foreign Office Spokesman dealing with the world's media. He is fascinated by the whole question of simulation and the representation of reality, about which he maintains a weblog (www.simulation.cc).

Foreword

Dr Yang-Im Lee

Westminster Business School, University of Westminster

In writing *Cyber Security Culture: Counteracting Cyber Threats through Organizational Learning and Training*, Peter Trim and David Upton have produced a book that will be of value to a range of professionals, as well as being of academic interest. Government officials, policy advisors, law enforcement officers and senior managers within companies are fully aware that cyber attacks are increasing in volume and that it is not always possible to devise a risk model that ensures that cyber and cyber related threats are dealt with in a satisfactory manner. The speed at which cyber related vulnerabilities are appearing, suggests that senior management throughout all industry sectors need to ensure that the organization invests adequately in security and has appropriate countermeasures in place. The business environment is undergoing rapid transformation and new cyber threats will materialize through time and in a rapidly changing and complex business environment, a fresh approach needs to be taken to skill development. It can be argued that it is no longer possible to train people to handle cyber threats in the way that training to manage other security threats has been done in the past, because the nature and complexity of the problem is growing in intensity.

Most managers do not fully understand information technology (IT) systems and certainly do not understand how these systems work and interlock with other IT systems. For example, IT networks are evolving so quickly that it is almost impossible for any one person to have a good understanding of every part of every system the organization uses and the new business models that are evolving are requiring managers to think more carefully about existing and future vulnerabilities.

One solution is for management to put tighter controls on the systems in place, such as more and more complex passwords, changed more often, with electronic updating systems that force employees to change their passwords. But this can easily become prohibitively time-consuming for the users, and also leads people to take shortcuts like writing passwords on Post-it notes, which make the new system less rather than more secure. This is the difference between what Chris Argyris has called 'espoused theories' and 'theories in use'. In other words, a reality check needs to be done to ensure that there is a logical fit between what an employee does and what they should do.

Another solution identified by senior management may be to train people to recognize attacks and respond to them. It can be argued that it is not useful practice to get everybody to use their initiative; for example, junior staff should use the security systems in place and obey the rules. But for others, it is much better to use some degree of initiative, especially in an entrepreneurial company where the emphasis is on rapid growth and quick reactions. Exercises are a good way of training people, especially since they involve group training and if the concept of organizational learning is embraced, a learning organization can materialize that promotes the development and the utilization of knowledge.

It can be argued that there is always a tension between the rule-bound systems and those who enforce them, and individuals of an entrepreneurial disposition will break the rules or find a way around them. Entrepreneurs and innovators invent rather than copy, and it should be noted that hackers and those implementing cyber-attacks, are innovators and highly knowledgeable about how complex systems can be penetrated. They are also hardened and persistent, and if they do not succeed the first time, will try again until they have found a way to exploit the vulnerability they have identified. One way through which this can be done is by gaining intelligence through various forms of social engineering.

It is possible to suggest ways in which the tension between the two sides of any organization is made into a 'creative tension', which develops understanding and helps the organization to learn (Argyris's second loop). Ideally the successful organization should have a two-loop model of training and operating in place, and this is what those countering the actions of cyber attackers need to advocate. It has already been shown in my own work with the authors of this volume that exercises help promote knowledge sharing, not just inside the organization but also between organizations. The Alternative Worlds research project from which this book stems provided additional insights and processes that will be beneficial in the fight against cyber crime. Research projects such as the one outlined in the book can do much to help provide encouragement and a means of helping managers in organizations to be more aware of the various cyber security threats and to be more proactive in their approach when dealing with them.

This valuable book provides an appreciation of the relevance of training exercises then looks at scenario planning, simulation exercises and the learning organization approach. Readers will be introduced to the Alternative Worlds project, the research and data collection processes it involved and the ethical issues that it raised. There are chapters on social engineering and on organizational and other issues relating to Critical Information Infrastructure Protection (CIIP). Approaches to analysis and modelling are described and insights into organizational learning are provided. This is all followed with a very practically focused section of the book that provides a road map for navigating through CIIP incidents and is accompanied by annexes relating to case studies and workshop scenarios.

The final chapters of the book address the change management and training and development aspects of the commended approach to cyber security, together with guidance on devising and implementing an effective strategy and policies. I fervently hope that this book will encourage managers to adopt a more systematic approach when putting cyber security systems in place and I am sure it will support them in that endeavour.

Preface

Cyber Security Culture: Counteracting Cyber Threats through Organizational Learning and Training has been written for a wide audience and will be of interest to academics, policy makers, practitioners, researchers and industry trainers. As well as being of direct use to ICT specialists, it will be of relevance to various functional managers as it covers in-depth a number of issues, such as how organizational learning can be used to produce cultural change within an organization so that the immediate cyber related threats facing the organization are dealt with. The authors believe that the speed and complexity of cyber attacks demand a different approach to security management, including scenario-based training, to supplement security polices and technical protection systems. The examples cited both inform and provide guidance for those responsible for securing systems within an organization and attempt to take a multi-approach view that addresses the behaviour of individuals as well as machines.

The book provides information that will help managers to form policy to prevent cyber intrusions. Guidance for counteracting current and future threats is provided. In particular, issues such as social engineering are addressed and placed in context. Although the work is embedded in a theoretical framework, non-ICT staff will find the book of practical use because although it deals with highly technical subjects, it attempts to make them accessible to the non-specialist reader and links firmly with human resource management issues that will allow the education–training divide to be bridged.

The research project referred to in this book was made possible through funding provided by the UK's Technology Strategy Board, under the Fast Track scheme associated with the Network Security – Information Infrastructure Protection programme, entitled 'Managing Complexity, Risk and Resilience'. The research project was entitled: 'Develop proven software system to improve emergency response exercises, and extend it to develop robustness in critical information infrastructure', and the project number was BKD59G TP 400124. The authors would like it to be known that they are highly appreciative and very grateful for the award that provided for the further development of Alternative Worlds and provided an opportunity to produce this book.

The authors would like to record their gratitude and thanks for research inputs and administrative tasks undertaken by Dr Yang-Im Lee and Mrs Gerti Hofmeister-Biddles during the life of the project. They would also like to thank the senior managers from various organizations in the private and public sectors, and independent advisors and policy makers who attended the workshops and participated in the data collection exercises, and provided additional assistance when asked to, all of which was extremely valuable.

Peter R.J. Trim and David Upton

1

Introduction and Background to the Research

1.0 Introduction

The authors of this book considered that as the research project involved studying subject matter that can be considered highly complex, it was necessary to view the research from the various perspectives outlined by Merriam (1988: 9) as they brought into focus the methodological issues: the nature and type of research questions posed; the amount of control the researchers possessed with respect to access to experts for example; and the nature and desired form of the end product (the main focus was upgrading the Alternative Worlds software product).

The chapter starts with an appreciation of the relevance of training exercises (Section 1.1) and this is followed by a brief look at scenario planning (Section 1.2). Simulation exercises and the learning organization approach are given consideration (Section 1.3) and the Alternative Worlds project is then placed in focus (Section 1.4). The methodological approach and the main steps in the research process (Section 1.5) are followed by the data collection process (Section 1.6). Ethical issues are given some consideration (Section 1.7) and a conclusion is then provided (Section 1.8).

1.1 The Relevance of Training Exercises

Exercises in this context are a means of stimulating a serious incident in order to train groups of people how to respond to a real incident. They are based as much as possible on reality in the sense that the exercise models 'real life' using detail drawn from real events to test how people would respond to a specific problem, allowing them to be trained to act in accordance with a particular response plan/set of plans (Upton 2009: 198). There are several types of exercises: table-top exercises are often small and cost effective, and allow participants to sit in the same room and, using visual devices such as slides or maps, work through a scenario (Lee et al. 2009: 727). A large-scale table-top exercise often involves role-playing, telephone communication and may incorporate physical simulation such as 'fire appliances may deploy to the scene of the imaginary incident and spray foam or rescue dummy casualties' (Lee et al. 2009: 727). Nowadays, table-tops can involve multi-national teams working simultaneously on a scenario and teleconferencing allows those involved to consult the same set of documents (Lee et al. 2009: 728). Computer links can ensure that decisions are fed to all those involved in the exercise, simultaneously and in real time. Larger scale exercises can involve actual simulation of events, using role-players, or mockups of attack signatures on personal computers (PCs).

The value of table-top exercises that utilize scenarios and which facilitate emergency planning has been outlined by Lasky (2010). Furthermore, table-top exercises based around a cyber-crime scenario are one method of posing questions about how managers and their subordinates should respond in a cyber attack. Different organizations will set different priorities and act differently, partly because they have different defence capabilities in place, as well as different vulnerabilities and cultures. Although organizations might respond in different ways, the training process should be consistent. The advantage of adopting a consistent approach to training to prevent cyber attacks, is that it allows those taking part in training exercises to measure themselves against standards, and helps them to identify the risk profile of their organization and their own department within the organization, making it easier to visualize and reduce the organization's overall vulnerability.

Immersing managers and their subordinates in a range of training exercises, helps to develop an 'exercise culture', in which personnel expect to be regularly tested on their crisis response skills and knowledge, in a non-threatening environment. Personnel who know what they would do if a crisis occurs will face it more calmly and more productively than those who do not. The results will be better. The company will be better able to demonstrate that it has compliance policies in place, and to justify its actions, if it is later called to account.

Other issues and problems that arise in real life can be built into the scenario and these can be multiple events and natural hazards that cause serious knock-on effects. In the case of a series of events occurring, it is useful to think in terms of a wider 'community' approach to crisis and disaster management, and it may be necessary for governments and international institutions to co-operate with respect to co-ordinating relief efforts as regards a certain disaster, and this suggests that multi-stakeholder partnerships are necessary in order to facilitate disaster and emergency management knowledge and also working practices that are underpinned by trust (Trim 2009: 219).

Evidence suggests that exercises allow those participating to gain greater familiarity with emergency response plans, to identify errors or shortcomings in plans or indeed operational procedures and to make contact with people working in a variety of organizations. This improves co-operation, decision-making and helps to raise the confidence level of those participating (Upton 2007: 84). Writing on the level and degree of interaction during a disaster/emergency, Trim and Lee (2007: 113) indicate that international co-operation takes many forms and often involves making available expertise and equipment, as well as financial support. A major disaster often witnesses co-operation among governments, institutions and organizations, and such co-operation usually results in the saving of life as well as better relations between nations.

A good summary of the techniques and objectives of scenario planning can be found in Schwartz (1992), one of the pioneers in the field. Schwartz (1992: 3) defines scenarios as:

> *a tool for helping us to take a long view in a world of great uncertainty ... [or] ... A tool for ordering ones perceptions about alternative future environments in which one's decisions might be played out.*

Scenario planning techniques have been used by major companies such as Shell, which regularly published scenarios for the future of the world's energy supply (see http://www.shell.com/home/content/aboutshell/our_strategy/shell _global_scenarios/). They have also been applied to industry sectors as a whole (for example, a report on a UK Institute of Petroleum scenario planning project jointly facilitated by Upton (1996)).

1.2   Scenario Planning

Scenario planning can be used by managers and strategists in particular to develop possible future worlds, which can then be used in training and educational settings. Indeed, scenario planning enables strategists to identify unique solutions to complex and recurring problems (Graetz 2002) and if coupled with simulation exercises, can improve an individual's decision-making skills (Feinstein et al. 2002: 733), and result in foresight and a continued commitment to training and staff development.

According to Trim and Lee (2008: 735):

> *Scenario planning forces senior managers to put in place a strategic monitoring system that enables the organization and its partners to formulate robust defensive strategies in times of uncertainty.*

It can also be argued that scenario planning forces managers to develop specialist knowledge by requiring them to find solutions to real problems (Lindgren and Bandhold 2003; Ringland 2006); however, Tessun (2001: 269) is right to suggest that those involved in scenario analysis need to be aware of the fact that senior managers do not always accept what are termed 'weak signals'. The consequences of this is that either more evidence has to be gathered relating to the circumstances or possible events identified (and this may be complicated in the case of a cyber attack owing to the fact that the people launching such an attack may not be based in the country from which the attack originates) and also, that a thorough risk assessment will be demanded if the threats identified are perceived as possibly yielding a low probability of occurrence but, if they materialize, may well have a high impact on the organization and the industry in which it competes.

1.3   Simulation Exercises and the Learning Organization Approach

Crookall and Thorngate (2009: 17) suggest that:

> *simulation/gaming would appear to provide a channel through which people may pass from knowledge to action and back again, to develop the two together hand in hand, to make action-knowledge one.*

The authors go on to state that:

> *The problem of learning from simulation/gaming lies not in simulation/gaming methods, nor in the difficulty of measuring change*

(i.e., learning), but simply in the inability of humans to translate their knowledge into positive and beneficial action, whether it be in simulation or in ordinary reality (Crookall and Thorngate 2009: 22–3).

Lee et al. (2009: 746) advocate an interdisciplinary approach to simulation and acknowledge that Crookall (2000: 11) is right to point out that:

Many simulation/games are interdisciplinary; the field of simulation/ gaming is interdisciplinary.

Simulation exercises can be used to develop our knowledge of organizational resilience and help managers to put in place various measures to ensure that any form of disaster is dealt with in a professional manner. Upton (2007: 72) has this to say on the subject:

Simulations are conducted by a range of authorities and agencies in the UK. In many cases they are required by law, or by operating conditions set by other bodies. Typically … the underlying legislation is brief, and only mentions a general obligation to take certain actions. This is supplemented by 'guidance', explaining the legislation and suggesting ways in which its requirements can be met. These guidances may be produced jointly by government and other bodies (local authorities, emergency services, and industry), or by government alone.

Reflecting on the comments above, it can be noted that simulation exercises can prove beneficial by preparing people to deal with a multi-faceted disaster (Trim 2006; Trim and Lee 2006; Trim and Lee 2007). Well designed and executed simulation exercises can help organizations in the public and private sectors to relate to each other better and to identify areas of activity that require joint action, such as disaster preparedness and after the event recovery for example. Lee et al. (2009: 741) acknowledge this and state that:

simulation designers and those in charge of organizing complex simulation exercises, can carefully monitor the performance of the participants and provide specific debriefings that allow those involved in the simulation exercise to reflect and better understand what experiential learning involves.

By thinking in terms of an experiential learning cycle, individuals can develop concrete experience, which is enriched by reflection, and this is 'given meaning by thinking, and transformed by action', and 'the new experience created becomes richer, broader, and deeper' (Kolb and Kolb 2008: 13). The key point to note is that an individual can interpret reality in a different way (Kriz 2003: 496), by thinking more deeply about what learning means to them. The advantage of this is that it will make an individual confident with respect to developing a skill base that is based on gaining knowledge about unknown situations. But is it as straightforward as that? Lee et al. (2009: 741) state that:

> organizations do not always learn from exercises. The US Congressional inquiry after the Hurricane Katrina flood in 2005 showed clearly that essential lessons from an earlier flood response exercise had not changed the organizations involved.

Possibly, the organizations involved considered the lessons learnt were for others to implement (Upton 2007), however, it is generally accepted that sharing lessons is important if the multiagency/'large' exercise is to achieve a number of objectives. It is also possible to suggest that learning is more difficult from a 'large' exercise/real large incident, as there is no single manager who can ensure that the information available is shared, and the responsibility for following up issues is assigned in the way that it should be. Budgetary, 'political' constraints and genuine misunderstandings, limit the willingness of each organization to take on new commitments or it can be argued make changes (Lee et al. 2009: 742), and this is something that has to be dealt with in the context of organizational learning.

Lee et al. (2009: 741) indicate that:

> For a learning organization culture to be established, it is essential that senior managers pay attention to how individuals learn and how they develop their skill and knowledge base.

Several factors contribute to how an individual learns and what stimulates an individual to absorb knowledge. Kolb and Kolb (2008: 9–10) acknowledge that most people do not 'understand their unique way of learning' and state that:

> Those individuals who believe that they can learn and develop have a learning self-identity. The learner faces a difficult challenge with a 'mastery response', while the person with a fixed identity is more likely to withdraw or quit. Learners embrace challenge, persist in the face of obstacles, learn from criticism, and are inspired by and learn from the

success of others. The fixed identity person avoids challenge, gives up easily, avoids criticism, and feels threatened by the success of others.

In his work on organizational learning, Argyris (1999) argues that the organization has to take the lead in establishing the right environment for organizational learning to take place, rather than simply prescribing rules or polices. Argyris (1999: 60 and 65) states:

> *The trouble with the old criteria is that they began and ended with behaviours. The new criteria begin with behaviour, in order to get a window into the mental maps and type of reasoning that the individuals use and the organisational culture that they create ... behaviours are crafted into action strategies that openly illustrate how the actors reached their evaluations or attributions and how they crafted them ... the premises are explicit, the inferences from the premises can also be made explicit.*

1.4   The Alternative Worlds Project

The project was designed to contribute directly to security and resilience in critical information infrastructures in all sectors of the UK economy, by making the response to major incidents more robust, resilient and rapid. The project extended the software system 'Alternative Worlds', which was licensed to a unit of a major oil company that used it to manage emergency response exercises in safety-critical areas. The support from the Technology Strategy Board (grant award BKD59G TP 400124) was much appreciated and allowed for the development of new algorithms that extended the data capabilites of the system. The funding also provided an opportunity for a social science perspective relating to aspects of cyber security to be developed. As a result, insights into human interaction and training in the area of emergency response planning and management were forthcoming. The work of Checkland and Scholes (2007) and Stevens (2011) was consulted at various times throughout the project and/or the writing-up stage.

The reason why the project was deemed important was because emergency response exercises are widely used in the UK and elsewhere to develop and test responses to incidents ranging from floods to major incidents and disasters such as the explosion at Buncefield. The exercise (or drill) is a means of simulating an incident so that the 'players' can practice and validate their response plans.

The management of stresses or failures in critical information infrastructure demands a complex response – not just from technicians but from all levels of management – and similar multi-disciplinary simulations.

There were several identifiable research objectives, including how to develop criteria and methodology for making exercises more effective, and how to improve the ways in which organizational specialists write and use them, using the 'Alternative Worlds' algorithms.

1.5 Methodological Approach and the Main Steps in the Research Process

The literature used throughout the research process was both specific and multi-disciplinary in nature, and was reviewed by both researchers. Trim, the co-researcher from the academic partner, attended a table-top exercise administered by Upton, the co-researcher from the company, prior to the first workshop at Birkbeck on 15 January 2010. Upton acted as the facilitator of the exercise, which was held on the premises of a major oil company. The table-top exercise was useful as it had a number of clearly defined objectives:

a) To provide training for site emergency response team.

b) To validate on-site emergency response plan.

c) To validate the off-site emergency response plan.

d) To practice liaison with the authorities and emergency services.

Trim wrote a report relating to the experience and insights gained from attending the table-top exercise and cross-checked matters against best practice outlined in the literature. As regards the relevancy of table-top exercises, the work of Lee et al. (2009) proved useful and Trim was able to make a link between theory and practice vis-à-vis using the table-top methodological approach in the context of a research project. It can be suggested that table-top exercises are relevant research methods as they allow unrelated material (through the process of experiencing) to be screened out (Wolcott 1992: 19–20). It can also be pointed out that the researchers engaged on the project were also conscious of the fact that they needed to maintain the support of the participants throughout the duration of the research project as their knowledge and expertise was considered essential to the success of the project. Policing by 'gatekeepers' was considered necessary as it allowed the participants to be involved in the research and to act as critical friends when necessary (Hammersley and Atkinson 1996: 63). Two other issues that were taken into consideration were the ethical way in which the research was conducted and the issue of fairness. Soltis (1996: 252–3) is right to highlight the fact that those that participate in research have their thoughts recorded and reported, and it was for this reason that the workshops were not tape-recorded. Indeed, the subject matter was considered highly sensitive as issues of national security and commercial confidentiality were touched upon and both the researchers agreed to operate within clearly defined constraints and not to put either an individual or an organization at risk.

1.6 The Data Collection Process

Several in-depth personal interviews (either face-to-face or over the telephone) were conducted at key points throughout the first six months of the research project. These were informal and somewhat conversational, and conformed to what Denzin (1989: 5–6) described as 'symbolic interaction'. Each interview lasted for about one hour on average, however, one face-to-face interview lasted for four hours as it was more broad based than the others and incorporated discussions relating to enhancing the image of the product and service, and other relevant user related topics and subjects. The in-depth personal interviews were deemed appropriate owing to the fact that the subject matter was highly complex and there were a number of known and unknown sensitivities that had to be dealt with. By keeping the interviews informal, it was possible to pose 'new' questions (Denzin 1989: 105) from time to time and this allowed the researchers to probe in depth when necessary and not to predetermine the outcome (Patton 1990: 13).

Those participating in the in-depth personal interviews also participated in some of the workshops. The workshop delegates were selected because of their knowledge and experience, and were in the main of senior or middle management rank. A number of participants had in fact worked in both the public and privates sectors, and some worked as independent consultants. It can be noted that about 25 per cent of the participants were from overseas, and each workshop had on average between 15 and 20 participants.

As regards the literature review, this was undertaken throughout the life of the project and was considered essential with respect to framing the table-top exercises that were used during the three workshops that were held at Birkbeck; and two shorter workshops that were held in Brussels (in conjunction with the European Corporate Security Association) and at Cranfield University/ Shrivenham. The scenarios developed for the hour-long *Exercising* component of the Technology Strategy Board – CAMIS conference held at Birkbeck on 28 June 2010, were also instrumental in the development of Alternative Worlds. The literature review provided insights into the subject matter and was used to underpin the writing of four reports (a positioning paper that was circulated to workshop attendees prior to workshop one (Birkbeck) and three additional reports, one of which stemmed from the deliberations of workshop one, and the other two were produced and circulated to the attendees prior to workshops two and three taking place). The logic behind providing those attending the workshops with reading material in advance was to enable the discussions during the workshops to proceed faster and to produce deeper insights that made the linking of theory and practice more obvious. This approach conformed to that outlined by Denzin (1989: 244), for example, the data collected from the small group interview (which was held at Birkbeck on 22 October 2010 prior to the workshop being held) and the questionnaire survey, which was distributed over a period of time at a number of the events outlined herewith, were used to verify comments, and the analysis and interpretation of the table-top exercises. It can be concluded therefore, that the research methods used during the research process allowed a holistic view to be taken of the subject (Patton 1990: 49) and that the data collected, analysed and interpreted, was valid and reliable.

As regards Workshop One (held at Birkbeck, University of London from 12.30pm to 4pm (preceded by lunch) on 15 January 2010), a positioning report entitled *Protecting Critical Information Infrastructure: Issues and Considerations*, was made available to those attending the workshop prior to the event (an edited version of the positioning paper forms Chapter 4 of this book). Three background notes were produced for the workshop and distributed accordingly and were used in the table-top exercise. Upton (acting as the facilitator) took those attending the workshop through the table-top exercises and three observers, including Trim, made notes on the content and interactions and supplied these to Upton shortly after the workshop. Soon after the workshop, a report entitled *Notes for a Report on Critical Information Infrastructure Protection*, was produced and circulated to those that had attended the workshop. An edited version of the report appears as Chapter 7 in this book.

Workshop Two (held at Birkbeck, University of London from 1pm to 4pm (preceded by lunch) on 29 March 2010), witnessed five background notes being used to underpin the table-top exercise. The background notes provided a focus for the discussions and were possibly more vibrant than those emanating from the first workshop. The facilitator, Upton, took those attending through the table-top exercises and three observers, including Trim, made notes on the content and interactions and supplied these to Upton soon after the workshop. A report entitled *Critical Information Infrastructure: Methods of Conceptualising Interdependencies that no-one Really Understands* was circulated prior to the workshop. An edited version of the report appears as Chapter 5 in this book.

The next Workshop was held in Brussels on 23 March 2010. The researchers presented a co-authored paper entitled 'Protecting Critical Information infrastructure: Keeping up with the threats'. The hosts were the European Corporate Security Association (ECSA) and 15 people were in attendance. The abstract of the paper presented read as follows (Trim and Upton 2010a):

> *Organizations all over the world are highly dependent on information technology. Electronic communication services and networks provide the backbone of the European economy and are vital to citizens, businesses and governments. The Protection of this Critical Information Infrastructure (CIIP) is universally acknowledged as a vital component of national security policy. In order to protect their critical infrastructure, most Western European countries have established sophisticated and comprehensive CIIP organizations and systems, involving governmental agencies from different ministries, with a variety of initiatives. These programmes try to cover all the different facets of CIIP, ranging from reducing vulnerabilities and fighting computer crime to defence against cyber-terrorism.*

Speaking to an audience including a range of experts with specialist knowledge in security, the researchers focused attention on cyber security threats that are confronting senior managers and government representatives, and provided examples of cyber security attacks. They looked at how senior managers in organizations might develop a culture of cyber security, given the increasing complexity they face. They also outlined how a new approach to information sharing and enhanced co-operation between organizations in research, education and training, would assist Critical Information Infrastructure Protection. The questionnaire referred to above was distributed and the data collected proved valuable in the context of the research project being undertaken relating to Alternative Worlds. As regards the table-top exercise, three scenarios were outlined and discussed in detail.

A fourth workshop was held at Cranfield University/Shrivenham on 3 June 2010. The researchers presented a co-authored paper entitled (Trim and Upton 2010b): 'Emergency response simulation system research: Research into cyber security – current and future issues and Alternative Worlds', to delegates attending the *Crisis Management Exercise Design and Development Workshop* at the Advanced Emergency Response Simulation System Research, Cranfield Resilience Centre, Cranfield University, Defence Academy of the United Kingdom. In their paper presentation, the researchers focused on a range of issues relating to cyber security and explained what their research into critical information infrastructure protection involved. Evidence relating to past disasters was drawn upon, including the Piper Alpha fire in 1988 and the Buncefield explosion in 2005, and links were made with modern day cyber threats. The topic of business continuity planning was given attention and so too were current and future threats posed by cyber-criminals. The theoretical and practical dimensions of the subject were brought together in a table-top exercise based around a cyber-crime scenario, which was composed of three stages. The ultimate aim of the exercise was to allow those present to think in terms of raising their awareness about risk and establishing how an 'exercise culture' could be established and solutions implemented. The presentation provided insights into the research being undertaken in relation to the 'Alternative Worlds' system, which was featured in CAMIS Newsletter Number 26 (vol. 6, no. 1). A main conclusion to emerge from the presentation was that there are an increasing number and type of cyber attacks on organizations and managers need to give more thought as to how information technology (IT) departments are to respond to both anticipated and unknown threats. Three scenarios were outlined and discussed in detail.

The Technology Strategy Board Project Portfolio and CAMIS Conference: 'Knowledge Sharing and Extending the Frontiers of Knowledge', which was held at Birkbeck, University of London, 28 June 2010, witnessed two paper presentations by Upton (one paper related to the Alternative Worlds project and another was a co-authored paper with a government representative (Upton and Powell 2010)). A one-hour *Exercising* session was included in the day's events and this allowed the participants to provide comments and assessments for certain types of scenario. The output was given to Upton and used in the development of Alternative Worlds.

The last workshop, Workshop Three (held at Birkbeck, University of London from 12.30pm to 4pm (preceded by lunch) on 22 October 2010) revolved around social engineering. A report entitled *Social Engineering* was made available to those attending the workshop prior to the event (an edited version of the report forms Chapter 2 of this book). Twelve scenarios were distributed for analysis and interpretation on the day, however, not all the scenarios were used owing to time constraints. Upton, who acted as the facilitator, took those attending through the table-top exercises and two observers, including Trim, made notes on the content and interactions. Trim related the discussions and especially the comments relating to training (which was covered in the report) to the discussions and made crosschecks with the small group interview case study narrative (contained in Chapter 6 of this book) and the output from the questionnaire survey (contained in Chapter 6 of this book). The small group interview, composed of five people, covered organizational learning, training and organizational value systems. It allowed Trim to probe and unravel 'cultural knowledge' (Spinder and Spinder 1992) relating to managing complex systems and how this manifested in social interaction (in particular policy formulation and the use and application of rules within organizations). A leading line of inquiry was how senior managers make and implement decisions in the context of the organization's value system and how organizations adapt to meet new challenges/threats. Workshop Three did in fact conclude the research project and allowed all the elements of the project to be brought together.

A questionnaire entitled 'Exercises and simulations of IT systems' was distributed to a range of experts on five separate occasions. For example, the questionnaire was distributed on three occasions at Birkbeck (the response rate was 4 out of 16 [the second workshop]; 4 out of 20 [TSB-CAMIS Conference]; and 1 out of 1 [in-depth interview with an industry expert], representing an overall response rate of 24 per cent). Although a higher number of people attended both the workshops and the TSB-CAMIS conference, some attended both events and were not required to complete the questionnaire more than once and some considered that the questionnaire was not relevant to their current role in the organization they worked for. One batch of the questionnaire was distributed to seven people attending a workshop at Cranfield University/ Shrivenham and all seven people completed the questionnaire (100 per cent response rate). One batch of the questionnaire was distributed to 11 people attending a workshop in Brussels and four people completed and returned the questionnaire representing a response rate of 36 per cent. A questionnaire survey was incorporated in the research strategy as this allowed extra data to be collected quickly from a wide range of experts. Furthermore, it was envisaged that minimum response error (Malhotra and Birks 2003: 326) would occur and this would make the research findings more robust.

It is worthwhile to note that Upton conducted eight table-top exercises during the research period and the analysis and interpretation of the table-top exercises were used in the development of the 'Alternative Worlds' software. It was evident during the workshops held as part of the 'Alternative Worlds' project that several questions recurred. Namely:

1.   How can security managers prioritize risks?

2.   How can strategists identify areas of future vulnerability?

3.   What type of business model needs to be devised in order to make an organization more robust?

4.   How can security managers ensure that the organization adopts a proactive approach to training and staff development?

An issue to emerge from the personal interviews, the small group interview, the workshops and the literature review, is that greater attention needs to be given to educating the public against being complacent in the sense that everybody is susceptible to a cyber attack, which could range from stealing somebody's identity and making purchases in their name to penetrating the controls of an electricity generating plant and closing it down. Hence the term 'security' needs to be more widely interpreted and more widely understood than it is at present, and security provision and training need to be more closely linked. By placing more emphasis on training, it is likely that security issues will be better understood, and all those affected will have a clearer understanding of the threats they face on a personal and corporate level.

1.7   Ethical Issues

A number of ethical issues were considered throughout the research process. For example, bearing in mind how sensitive the topic was and how important it was to avoid addressing national security issues, it was decided that none of the workshops would be tape-recorded and that if at any point in the proceedings a sensitive issue arose, that every precaution would be taken not to expose classified data or information. (Only the small group interview was tape-recorded and each member was provided with a copy of the case study narrative once it had been produced so that they could verify the content.) By paying attention to how the discussions were developing, it can be argued that none of the participants were placed in an embarrassing situation (Malhotra and Birks 2003: 173). Prior to a workshop being conducted, an invitation was sent to each prospective delegate outlining the rules of engagement and this had a positive effective of keeping the participants committed to the project. It can also be suggested that the injects deployed during the table-top exercises were used in a logical and controlled manner.

1.8   Conclusion

Training exercises take many forms and can be deemed necessary with respect to countering the growing types of cyber threats that can be considered costly both in terms of time expended and the cost of the resource(s) involved. Indeed, in order to prepare the workforce for eventualities such as prolonged and persistent cyber attacks, senior management need to invest more heavily in devising and deploying simulation exercises that incorporate realistic scenarios and which reinforce an organization's commitment to becoming and sustaining a learning organization culture. As well as investing in traditional forms of training and education, it is also necessary for research to be undertaken to establish a more theoretical base upon which training and staff development programmes can be based, and the role that virtual learning devices play with respect to knowledge transfer and the enhancement of an individual's skill base. Although there are various forms of training available to companies, as regards complex and dynamic situations, it is useful to think in terms of utilizing the table-top exercise approach so that the scenarios developed and worked with contain the necessary detail for those involved in the decision-making process to fine tune their decision-making capabilities. By placing training within a group context, it should be possible for the participants to develop a holistic view and embrace innovative ways to solve problems, and at the same time learn how to be sensitive to the feelings and concerns of others, which are very important factors with respect to managing emergencies and dealing with people's sensitivities.

List of Definitions

An *observer* is an 'exercise participant who watches selected segments as they unfold, whilst remaining separate from player activities' (BSI 2010: 3).

An *exercise* is a 'planned rehearsal of a possible incident designed to evaluate an organization's capability to manage that incident and to provide an opportunity to improve the organization's future responses and enhance the relevant competences of those involved' (BSI 2010: 3).

A *simulation* is an 'exercise in which a group of players, usually representing a control centre or management team, react to a simulated incident notionally happening elsewhere' (BSI 2010: 3).

A *table-top exercise* is a 'facilitated exercise in which participants are given specific roles to perform, either as individuals or groups' (BSI 2010: 4).

A *facilitator* is a 'person who presents the scenario of a seminar or table-top exercise to the players and helps to bring about a successful conclusion to the exercise by giving unobtrusive guidance, helping the players to solve problems or communicating problems and taking feedback, without becoming involved in the players' actual discussions' (BSI 2010: 4).

An *inject* is a 'scripted piece of information input to the exercise designed to elicit a response or decision and facilitate the flow of the exercise' (BSI 2010: 4).

A *player* is an 'exercise participant who responds to a set of stimuli generated by the exercise script' (BSI 2010: 4).

A *scenario* is a 'pre-planned storyline that drives an exercise and is chosen to enable it to meet its objectives' (BSI 2010: 4).

References

Argyris, C. 1999. *On Organisational Learning*. Malden, MA: Blackwell.

BSI. 2010. *PD 25666:2010 Business Continuity Management – Guidance on Exercising and Testing for Continuity and Contingency Programmes*. London: British Standards Institute.

CAMIS Newsletter 2010. Number 26 (Volume 6, Issue 1). London: Birkbeck, University of London/CSCEO Management Services Limited.

Checkland, P. and Scholes, J. 2007. *Soft Systems Methodology in Action*. Chichester: John Wiley & Sons, Ltd.

Crookall, D. 2000. Thirty years of interdisciplinarity [Editorial]. *Simulation & Gaming*, 31 (1), 5–21.

Crookall, D. and Thorngate, W. 2009. Acting, knowing, learning, simulating, gaming [Editorial]. *Simulation & Gaming,* 40 (1), 8–26.

Denzin, N.K. 1989. *The Research Act: A Theoretical Introduction to Sociological Methods.* Englewood Cliffs, NJ: Prentice Hall, Inc.

Feinstein, A.H., Mann, S. and Corsun, D.L. 2002. Charting the experiential territory: Clarifying definitions and uses of computer simulations, games and role play. *Journal of Management Development,* 21 (10), 732–44.

Graetz, F. 2002. Strategic thinking versus strategic planning: Towards understanding the complementarities. *Management Decision,* 40 (5), 456–62.

Hammersley, M. and Atkinson, P. 1996. *Ethnography: Principles and Practice.* London: Routledge.

Kolb, A.Y. and Kolb, D.A. 2008. The learning way: Meta-cognitive aspects of experiential learning. Simulation. *Simulation & Gaming.* Available at: http://www.learningfromexperience.com/research-library/ [accessed: 5 March 2009].

Kriz, W.C. 2003. Creating effective learning environments and learning organizations through gaming simulation design. *Simulation & Gaming,* 34 (4), 495–511.

Lasky, M. 2010. The value of table-top exercises and one-page planning documents. *Journal of Business Continuity & Emergency Planning,* 4 (2), 132–41.

Lee, Y-I., Trim, P.R.J., Upton, J. and Upton, D. 2009. Large emergency-response exercises: Qualitative characterizes – a survey. *Simulation & Gaming,* 40 (6), 726–51.

Lindgren, M. and Bandhold, H. 2003. *Scenario Planning,* Basingstoke: Palgrave Macmillan.

Malhotra, N.K. and Birks, D.F. 2003. *Marketing Research: An Applied Approach.* Harlow: Pearson Education Limited.

Merriam, S.B. 1988. *Case Study Research in Education: A Qualitative Approach.* San Francisco, CA: Jossey-Bass Publishers.

Ringland, G. 2006. *Scenario Planning.* Chichester: John Wiley & Sons, Ltd.

Schwartz, P. 1992. *The Art of the Long View.* London: Century Business.

Stevens, R. 2011. *Engineering Mega-Systems: The Challenge of Systems Engineering in the Information Age.* Boca Raton, FL: CRC Press/Taylor & Francis Group.

Patton, M.Q. 1990. *Qualitative Evaluation and Research Methods.* Newbury Park, CA: Sage Publications, Inc.

Soltis, J.F. 1996. The ethics of qualitative research, in *Education,* edited by E.W. Eisner and A. Peshkin. New York, NY: Teachers College Press, 247–57.

Spinder, G. and Spinder, L. 1992. Cultural process and ethnography: An anthropological perspective, in *The Handbook of Qualitative Research in Education,* edited by M.N. LeCompte, et al. San Diego, CA: Academic Press, Inc., 53–92.

Tessun, F. 2001. Scenario analysis and early warning systems at Daimler-Benz Aerospace, in *Proven Strategies in Competitive Intelligence: Lessons from the Trenches*, edited by J.E. Prescott and S.H. Miller. New York, NY: John Wiley & Sons, Inc., 259–73.

Trim, P.R.J. 2006. Disaster and emergency scenarios: Pointers for educationalists, trainers and practitioners, in *The International Simulation and Gaming Yearbook Volume 14: Simulations and Games for Risk, Crisis and Security Management*, edited by E. Borodzicz. Edinburgh: Society for the Advancement of Games and Simulations in Education and Training (SAGSET), 111–19.

Trim, P.R.J. 2009. Placing disaster management policies and practices within a stakeholder security architecture, in *Strategizing Resilience and Reducing Vulnerability*, edited by P.R.J. Trim and J. Caravelli. New York, NY: Nova Science Publishers Inc., 213–27.

Trim, P.R.J. and Lee, Y-I. 2006. A multi-cultural communication model to be used in disaster and emergency management simulation exercises, in *The International Simulation and Gaming Yearbook Volume 14: Simulations and Games for Risk, Crisis and Security Management*, edited by E. Borodzicz. Edinburgh: Society for the Advancement of Games and Simulations in Education and Training (SAGSET), 120–30.

Trim, P.R.J. and Lee, Y-I. 2007. An extended multi-cultural communication model for use in disaster and emergency simulation exercises, in *The International Simulation & Gaming Research Yearbook Volume 15: Effective Learning From Games & Simulations*, edited by P.R.J. Trim and Y-I Lee. Edinburgh: Society for the Advancement of Games and Simulations in Education and Training (SAGSET), 108–18.

Trim, P.R.J. and Lee, Y-I. 2008. A strategic marketing intelligence and multi-organisational resilience framework. *European Journal of Marketing*, 42 (7/8), 731–45.

Trim, P.R.J. and Upton, D. 2010a. Protecting Critical Information Infrastructure: Keeping up with the Threats, European Corporate Security Association (ECSA) Academy, Dolce La Hulpe, Brussels, Belgium, 23 March 2010.

Trim, P.R.J. and Upton, D. 2010b. Emergency Response Simulation System Research: Research into Cyber Security – Current and Future Issues and Alternative Worlds, *Crisis Management Exercise Design and Development Workshop – Advanced*, Cranfield Resilience Centre, Cranfield University, Shrivenham, 3 June 2010.

Upton, D. 1996. *Waves of Fortune*. Chichester: John Wiley & Sons, Ltd.

Upton, D. 2007. Official crisis simulations in the UK and elsewhere, in *The International Simulation & Gaming Research Yearbook Volume 15: Effective Learning From Games & Simulations*, edited by P.R.J. Trim and Y-I Lee.

Edinburgh: Society for the Advancement of Games and Simulations in Education and Training (SAGSET), 70–88.

Upton, D. 2009. Some suggestions for making emergency response exercises more consistent and more successful, in *Strategizing Resilience and Reducing Vulnerability*, editors P.R.J. Trim and J. Caravelli. New York, NY: Nova Science Publishers, Inc., 197–212.

Upton, D. and Powell, A. 2010. Critical Information Infrastructure Protection and Information Sharing. *The Technology Strategy Board Project Portfolio and CAMIS Conference: 'Knowledge Sharing and Extending the Frontiers of Knowledge'*, Birkbeck, University of London, London, 28 June 2010.

Wolcott, H.F. 1992. Posturing in qualitative inquiry, in *The Handbook of Qualitative Research in Education*, edited by M.N. LeCompte. San Diego, CA: Academic Press, Inc., 3–52.

Websites

See http://www.shell.com/home/content/aboutshell/our_strategy/shell_global _scenarios/ [accessed: 2010]

2

Social Engineering

2.0 Introduction

The authors of this book are convinced that the complexities associated with cyber security demand that a fresh approach is taken with respect to improving security generally. Improving and expanding security education is considered a must if the problems identified are to be dealt with in a timely manner. Possibly a more radical approach has to be taken to improving security awareness and education, and this means understanding better the motives of those that launch cyber attacks. Education and training are distinct; however, training should be given more prominence as it is aimed at developing judgement. In this chapter, reference is made to the size of the problem (Section 2.1), to social engineering (Section 2.2) and to who does it and why (Section 2.3). Attention is then given to targets: the employees (Section 2.4), what happens in the real world (Section 2.5) and then a conclusion is provided (Section 2.6).

2.1 The Size of the Problem

It is common knowledge that the number of IT security breaches being detected, and the cost of fixing them, is growing. For instance, a survey by PricewaterhouseCoopers (PwC 2010a, Executive Summary: 4) found that 92 per cent of large organizations reported an information security breach in 2009/2010, as opposed to 72 per cent in 2008. The average cost of handling each incident rose to between £280,000 to £690,000 in 2010. (In 2008 it was between £90,000 and £170,000.)

PwC make only one reference to 'social engineering' in its report, though Andrew Beard, director of OneSecurity at PwC (PwC 2010b) said:

> Part of the solution to ensure better security is encrypting data and we see that there has been huge improvements in this area with regard

*to laptops, USB sticks and other removable media ... But educating
people is just as important and more companies than ever before now
have a security policy, although only 19% of respondents from large
organisations believed their policy is very well understood by staff. The
root cause of this is that investment in security awareness training,
while on the increase, is still often inadequate.*

A survey by Verizon (2010), based on their own and US Secret Service data,
suggests that:

- 48 per cent of data breaches were caused by insiders. (Some 10 per
  cent of these were due to 'policy violations and other questionable
  behavior that, while not overtly malicious, can still result in harm
  to information assets'; the remaining 90 per cent were due to
  'deliberate and malicious' activity). (Verizon note that 'Not only
  can inappropriate behavior contribute directly to a breach, but it
  may also be an ill omen of what's to come. Over time investigators
  have noticed that employees who commit data theft were often
  cited in the past for other "minor" forms of misuse'.)

- 27 per cent involved multiple parties.

- 48 per cent involved privilege misuses ('using organizational
  resources or privileges for any purpose or in a manner contrary to
  that which was intended').

- 28 per cent employed social tactics ('deception, manipulation,
  intimidation, etc. to exploit the human element, or users, of
  information assets. These actions are often used in conjunction
  with other categories of threat (i.e. malware designed to look like
  antivirus software) and can be conducted through technical and
  non-technical means').

Verizon (2010) adds that:

- 85 per cent of the attacks were not considered highly difficult.

- 96 per cent of breaches were avoidable through simple or
  intermediate controls, although: 'The proportion of breaches
  stemming from highly sophisticated attacks remained rather low

yet once again accounted for roughly nine out of ten records lost'. In other words, the most damaging attacks tend to be the most sophisticated.

There have been several high-profile examples of what appear to be 'disgruntled employee' breaches recently, for example:

1.   The leak of personal details of 170,000 employees and contractors from a Shell internal database (Pagnamenta 2010).

2.   The leak of some 90,000 classified US government documents about the war in Afghanistan to Wikileaks and a group of international newspapers (*The Guardian* 2010).

However, our focus in this chapter is on the well-meaning employee, and how to protect him or her from inadvertently causing an Information Security breach, usually in response to a 'social engineering' attack.

2.2   What is 'Social Engineering'?

Wikipedia (2010a) offers a simple definition:

> *Social engineering is the act of manipulating people into performing actions or divulging confidential information, rather than by breaking in or using technical cracking techniques; essentially a fancier, more technical way of lying. While similar to a confidence trick or simple fraud, the term typically applies to trickery or deception for the purpose of information gathering, fraud, or computer system access; in most cases the attacker never comes face-to-face with the victim.*

Davis (2007: 181) states that:

> *Social Engineering has been defined in numerous ways. The best definition is an enemy who manipulates or uses psychological tricks to gain the confidence of an authorized network employee relying on the natural human tendency to trust and help others. While there may be internal, disgruntled enemies within your organizational system, the external enemy will, more than likely, use social engineering to terrorize your organization. These hackers will rely on the fact that*

*people within your organization are either willing to share private
information or are unaware of the value of information they possess and
therefore are careless about protecting it.*

Harley (1998: 9) offers the following definition: 'Psychological manipulation,
skilled or otherwise, of an individual or set of individuals to produce a desired
effect on their behaviour'. This definition does not specifically distinguish
between confidence tricks or frauds involving computers, and those that do not.
However, the techniques are the same. Only the scenarios and the objectives
may differ.

The (unintentional) guru of social engineers is undoubtedly Robert
Cialdini (1993), Regents' Professor Emeritus of Psychology and Marketing at
Arizona State University, whose book, *Influence*, has sold over 2 million copies
and been translated into 26 languages. The book identifies six 'Weapons of
Influence' and, for convenience, and to demonstrate that even sophisticated
people still fall for these techniques on a huge scale, four examples (see Table
2.1) have been chosen from media reporting of a recent high-profile incident
of financial social engineering, the investment 'Ponzi scheme' promoted by
Bernie Madoff.

Table 2.1   High profile incident of financial social engineering

Professor Cialdini's weapons	Madoff's marketing techniques
Social proof (do things you see other people doing).	Deals were struck in steakhouses and at charity events, sometimes by Mr Madoff himself, but with increasing frequency by friends acting on his behalf. 'In a social setting – that's where it always happened', said Jerry Reisman, a lawyer from Garden City, NY, who knew Mr Madoff socially. 'Country clubs, golf courses, locker rooms. Recommendations, word of mouth. That's how it was done'.
Authority (natural tendency to obedience to superiors or experts).	Madoff had a good track record (e.g. on NASDAQ Board of Governors). 'Everyone was in awe of him', said Jerry Reisman, an attorney who met Madoff at a party. 'Madoff made it feel as if it was an exclusive club, and that's how he sucked his people in. That's how he got them to go into this. And it was a fantastic, brilliant job of marketing'.
Liking the person: people are easily persuaded by other people that they like, or feel are similar to themselves.	'He appeared to believe in family, loyalty and honesty', said one former Madoff employee, who asked to remain anonymous because of the continuing litigation and investigations. 'Never in your wildest imagination would you think he was a fraudster'.

Table 2.1   Continued

Professor Cialdini's weapons	Madoff's marketing techniques
Scarcity: perceived scarcity, urgency.	Dozens of now-outraged Madoff investors recall that special lure — the sense that they were being allowed into an inner circle, one that was not available to just anyone. A lawyer would call a client, saying: 'I'm setting up a fund for Bernie Madoff. Do you want in?' Or an accountant at a golf club might tell his partner for the day: 'I can make an introduction. Let me know'.
Reciprocation: 'we should try to repay what another person has provided for us'.	
Consistency 'our nearly obsessive desire to be consistent with what we have already done'.	

There are many techniques used by 'social engineers'. The following list (see Table 2.2) is by no means finite. It is based on work by Harley (1998), Mitnick (2002) and Whitaker et al. (2009). Use of Cialdini's (1993) techniques is clear.

Table 2.2   List of social engineering approaches

Technique	Example or explanation
Just ask:	It is amazing what some people will tell you if you just ask them nicely, particularly if you do not ask any one individual too many questions.
Build trust:	Try to develop a rapport with the target.
Offer to help (e.g. solve a problem you caused?):	Create or exploit an issue which causes them a problem, then offer to solve it (in order to do this, you need a small amount of information from them ...).
Get sympathy, ask for help:	Tell a hard-luck story – you are a field engineer, have lost your password file, need to clear up a major issue for an important client, boss on your back, wife going into hospital, can they just tell you the password ...
Use guilt or intimidation:	Your colleague promised to tell me this; I am a major customer, etc. Or I am the CEO's new personal assistant – he is waiting for this right now, about to do a TV interview, etc.
Reverse sting – get them to call you:	Claim to be the help desk of a supplier aware of a new virus. Give them your number in case it happens. Create a minor systems issue (perhaps by a technical attack). Wait for them to call.
Attack entry-level employees:	New or very junior employees are likely to be less well trained and more vulnerable to intimidation by supposed 'senior managers'. Also, they are unlikely to know individuals personally or recognize their voices, making impersonation easier.

Table 2.2   Continued

Technique	Example or explanation
Malicious mischief, bomb threats, faked communications:	Creating an incident (e.g. a bomb threat) to put everyone under pressure at the moment you call, distracting them and making them more likely to try to give you what you want in order to get you off the line.
Using targeted e-mails or calls ('spear-phishing'):	Using your knowledge of the organization to create a situation (e-mail or call) which the recipient expects: impersonating a genuine contact or request, sending genuine data of interest to the organization, but including a virus.

These methods can be used in a variety of 'attack vectors' (see Table 2.3).

Table 2.3   Attack vectors

Vector	Typical scenario	Typical objective
Virtual interaction	Devising a plausible e-mail which tempts the target to load software.	Induce the target to load malware.
Telephone	Getting information from a switchboard operator or junior staff member.	Build up information to facilitate another form of attack.
Physical contact	Making legitimate visits and picking up information, by talking or looking around.	As above.
'Dumpster diving'	Derive information from waste, eg paper waste, old disks, old PCs, or other 'thrown away' sources.	As above.
Covert intrusion	Making unauthorized visits, to pick up information or to attack systems.	Build up information, or introduce hostile code, either on USB sticks or directly.
Third party	Inducing a third party, with legitimate access, to misuse it.	Any of the above.

More or less legitimate tools are also used for research – e.g., looking at the target's website to find out what system is hosting it, using social networking sites or the trade press to find out names of staff, or current issues the target is following.

If the target site has made any obvious security mistakes, these can sometimes be picked up using tools like Goolag, which automatically scans for such errors, known as 'Google dorks'. (Please note that it is possible the use of this tool is an offence within the UK, under the Computer Misuse Act 1990 as amended by the Police and Justice Act 2006.)

2.3   Who Does This, and Why?

A taxonomy of hackers is provided in Table 2.4. They range from the very sad to the very dangerous.

Table 2.4   **Taxonomy of hackers**

Hacker	Abilities	Motivation	Impact of successful attack
Official: penetration testers, security companies, your own network managers.	High, hopefully.	Respectable.	Positive (should lead to security enhancement).
Criminals: identity thieves, confidence tricksters, people simply out to steal from you.	Anywhere from low to high – but the software can now be easily bought by non-experts (Reuters 2010).	Ordinary crime, e.g. theft, fraud.	May be serious. Likely to show up eventually in accounts, etc.
Commercial espionage: unscrupulous rivals, sales forces, and recruiters.	Anywhere from low to high.	To obtain business information: plans, IP, etc. Some evidence that this is done on a national basis – e.g. state agency actor, to give national companies advantages in negotiations.	Possibly very high, but may never be noticed except as series of unsuccessful negotiations, being undercut, products being copied, etc.
Private detectives, information brokers, Individuals.	Likely to be good at 'social engineering'.	Often following up personal cases.	High threat to your obligations to protect personal data.
Personal: 'script kiddies', disgruntled low-level employees.	Varied, but if high often narrowly limited in scope.	Personal satisfaction. May seek to crash or disfigure your systems, e.g. the US-based 'Iranian Cyber Army' (Zone-h 2010).	Usually limited to minor annoyance. Likely to be quickly apparent. The worst danger is possibly from unintended consequences!
Activists: political, social.	Varies. May be extremely sophisticated and motivated.	Single-issue support (e.g. perception that you are damaging the environment).	Most likely to cause embarrassment than steal money. Likely to be exploited quickly.
State: cyber-warfare, political intelligence-gathering, economic intelligence-gathering.	May be exceptionally high.	At worst, potential sabotage in times of strife. Or to give national companies a commercial edge – see above.	May go unnoticed for some time. May have very serious impact.

The 'social engineer' is usually trying to find information, as part of an attack process. When enough information has been built up, usually from several sources, the technical attack can be launched. Mitnick (2002: 264), himself a famous (now reformed) 'social engineer', lists four types of information that he typically sought in the attacks which earned him his fame (and five years' imprisonment):

1. **Confidential:** *trade secrets, IPR data, financial data, strategic plans, not disclosed widely even within the company.*

2. **Private:** *personal information about individuals that could allow attacks on them or embarrass them if leaked (and would lead to DPA fines).*

3. **Internal:** *general information about how the organisation works: organograms, general security procedures, system information. This is the most difficult category to define and the most vulnerable. People may not understand that some data is sensitive, and it is often possible to put two or three pieces of innocent internal data together to produce something much more useful than the sum of the parts. (For example, the author once observed his bank manager identify himself over the telephone to another manager from a different branch of the same bank, by quoting a number derived from a simple formula relating to the page of the bank's internal directory on which the second manager was listed. Junior staff who were unaware of this practice might easily be persuaded to tell a plausible attacker the page number on which a target person was listed – perhaps under the excuse of checking that they have the up-to-date version of the directory.)*

4. **Public:** *information that can be freely disclosed.*

Much of Mitnick's (2002) book elaborates the point that attacks on 'internal' data (section 3) are the most difficult to handle, since this data is often not obviously sensitive. The attacker may approach different people under different disguises, and elucidate one apparently harmless piece of information from each. Put together, however, these pieces can build up a much larger pattern. Once obtained, the individual pieces of information are processed to 'enumerate' the target.

Slade (2010: 7), building on work by Solove, refers to the impact of five types of 'information processing' as they affect personal privacy. At least four of these categories are relevant to attacks on organizations – for instance:

- Aggregation: the combination of various pieces of data about a person. The same technique is used to build up an attack on organizations by combining data about internal procedures and systems.

- Identification: linking information to particular individuals. Similarly, individuals can be linked to organizations and organizations to each other, for example to identify suppliers and customers.

- Insecurity: carelessness in protecting stored information from leaks and improper access. This is an issue particularly for infrastructure operators who handle data about or belonging to other organizations.

- Secondary use: the use of collected information, for a purpose different from the use for which it was collected, without the data owner's consent.

Slade's (2010) fifth category is exclusion: 'concerns the failure to allow the data subject to know about the data that others have about her and participate in its handling and use'. Obviously an attacker does not usually alert his target to the use he is making of its data. However, it is interesting to note in this context the asymmetry of many information sources. To give one example, many business people use the 'LinkedIn' social network. Basic access to this is free; paid access brings extra privileges, in exchange for a monthly fee. For example, LinkedIn regularly tells you if anyone has looked at your personal profile. For a free subscriber this takes the form of a 'teaser' saying something like 'Your profile has been viewed by 7 people in the past 15 days', with a hyperlink to a page giving general details about these viewers. (For example, 'Someone in the Design industry from London, United Kingdom'.) However, paying subscribers can actually see the names of the people who have viewed their sites. (Non-paying users viewing a target's personal pages have no way of knowing if their target will be able to find out their own name.) This 'asymmetry' is an example of Slade's (2010) fifth category, but whether you enjoy the 'right' to know who has looked at your site depends solely on whether you pay a subscription, not on any inherent 'fairness' of access or 'rights'.

Mitnick (2002), Whitaker et al. (2009), and others give fascinating examples of how data is processed to build up an attack. There are also media reports of activities by other famous hackers – e.g., the Badir Brothers (Wired 2002),

Adrian Lamo (Wikipedia 2010b), the 'Yes Men' (Wikipedia 2010c) and the Chaos Computer Club (Wikipedia 2010d). A subculture has built up around the activity, which deserves a proper psychological and sociological study. The damage caused can be severe (CNET 2003; ZDNet 2003; ComputerWorld 2010).

As an additional example of a (probably nationally co-ordinated) 'commercial' attack, reports suggest that senior executives in three major US oil companies received 'spear-phishing' e-mails, apparently from genuine contacts and with plausible contents (Wired 2010):

> *Marathon Oil first became suspicious when, on Nov. 13, 2008, a senior executive in the company's Houston office received an e-mail that appeared to be a reply to a message she had sent a corporate colleague overseas. The original message, which included a URL, related to the U.S. government's bailout plan for U.S. banks. The executive did not send the original message and warned colleagues to avoid the e-mail if they received one.*

The URL linked to a Trojan, which appears to have sent data from the target system to computers overseas, including one in China. The article speculates that the attackers were looking for 'bid data' – the companies' assessment of potential oil-bearing blocks, for which they might be making bids in international auctions. This is a classic case of taking 'internal' or 'public' data (the names and e-mail addresses of executives, the type of issue they might be discussing via e-mail) and processing them to 'build trust', and to make a technical attack possible. The value to a rival oil company could be considerable, and the national strategic advantage of gaining control of foreign oil resources would also be high.

As well as Mitnick's (2002) four categories of information, four additional categories can be added:

1. Safety: information which could affect safety systems, either allowing an attacker to damage them, or allowing a virus to infect them.

2. Operational: information which could be used to affect or halt company operations

3. Process: information involving SCADA or process control systems.

4.   Third-party: information carried, stored or processed on behalf of third parties. The carrier or processor has no way of assessing which parts of it are sensitive and which are 'public'.

These types of information are particularly relevant to Critical Information Infrastructure providers, who bear an additional responsibility to third parties if their systems fail. Three examples at random:

1.   El Pais (2010) records enquiry evidence that an air crash which killed 154 people in 2008 would not have occurred if Spanair computers had not been infected by a Trojan, causing maintenance data to be unavailable, so that the aircraft took off with unsolved faults, which may have directly caused it to crash. (Which malware was involved has not been made public, but the use of the word 'Trojan' suggests that the infection involved a human mistake.)

2.   Although this is not generally accepted, the Stuxnet worm has been blamed for a failure in the Indian communications satellite which affected about 70 per cent of direct-to-home (DTH) customers across the country in July 2010. Stuxnet may spread through USB sticks (SIFY 2010).

3.   Manchester was unable to issue parking tickets for a while in 2009, because of the Conficker worm (Register 2009). The infection was apparently caused by the use of memory sticks.

The economic impact of infrastructure failures is likely to be high (see Dynes et al. 2006), but 'traditional' analyses of infrastructure systems failures tend not to look for 'social engineering'. For example, Rahman et al. (2009) analyse their data using categories such as:

•   Hardware fault: all fault classes that affect hardware.

•   Software fault: fault caused by an error in the software system.

•   Human error: non-deliberate faults introduced by a mistake.

•   Malicious logic fault: these include Trojan horses, logic or timing bombs, viruses, worms, zombies or DoS attack.

- Authorization violation: attempt by an unauthorized person to access
  or damage network resources, but does not exclude the possibility of
  authorized users who are exceeding their rights. This also includes
  unauthorized sharing of digital contents, like audio, video or software.

The highly publicized advent of the Stuxnet worm may force a revision of this
approach, since it seems clear that 'social engineering' techniques went into the
construction of this worm, as well as its introduction into highly specific target
systems.

It is worth pointing out that much code for use in attacks is readily available
over the internet – Goolag, for example. Sometimes this is overtly offered as
'underground' material – see for instance the Cult of the Dead Cow website
(CDC 2010). Sometimes it is offered as reputable tools for 'reverse engineers'
and 'white hat' hackers – i.e. people who try to find vulnerabilities in their own
code in order to close them. The Immunity Debugger, for example, is described
on its website as 'A debugger with functionality designed specifically for the
security industry', but also as 'a powerful new way to write exploits. Cuts
exploit development time by 50%' (Immunity 2010).

As well as online hacking 'magazines' such as *Phrack* (Wikipedia 2010e)
there are hard-copy magazines such as *2600* (Wikipedia 2010f). Mainstream
publishers now issue books which are at best 'grey hat' material – e.g., *The
Best of 2600: A Hacker Odyssey* published by Wiley in 2008, and *Gray Hat Python*
published by the No Starch Press in 2009. The latter gives detailed instructions
on how, for example, to find vulnerabilities in Windows, and specimen code to
automate this process.

While much of this is highly technical material and is 'computer engineering'
rather than 'social engineering', it makes technical attacks much more accessible
to would-be hackers and encourages the use of 'social engineering' to close the
gaps.

2.4   Targets: The Employees

Employees may be considered under several headings:

1. Reception/switchboard/security. These are often the first point of
   contact with the company for an attacker, or for the public. They

have considerable access to 'internal' and 'safety' information. Socially, in many cases they are junior staff, often contractors with no especial loyalty to the organization at whose premises they work, and likely to be short-term or temporary employees. Sadly in many organizations they are often not encouraged to integrate fully and feel part of the team.

2.   Help desks and IT support staff. As Harley (1998: 18) points out:

> IT staff in general both pose and are vulnerable to special risks. They're often assumed to have a wider range of knowledge than is really appropriate. Even worse, they're under pressure to reinforce that view of themselves, not only to bolster their own self-image, but to reflect well on the unit of which they're part. They may have privileged access to particular systems (but not expert knowledge of those systems, necessarily). They are often encouraged to experiment, and are usually expected to teach themselves as much as possible. It's no coincidence that IT staff constitute a classic virus vector, either: in the absence of proper controls, they are apt to flit from user to user without taking elementary precautions ... team members make tempting targets for social engineering attacks.

Verizon (2010: 18) states:

> While it is clear that pulling off an inside job doesn't require elevated privileges, evidence consistently supports that they do facilitate the bigger ones. Overall, insiders were not responsible for a large share of compromised records but system and network administrators nabbed most of those that were. This finding is not surprising since higher privileges offer greater opportunity for abuse. In general, we find that employees are granted more privileges than they need to perform their job duties and the activities of those that do require higher privileges are usually not monitored in any real way.

3.   Senior managers. Senior managers have wide access to confidential information. Verizon (2010: 18) states:

> *It is worth noting that while executives and upper management were not responsible for many breaches, IP and other sensitive corporate information was usually the intended target when they were. These acts were often committed after their resignation or termination. Speaking of that, across all types of internal agents and crimes, we found that 24% was perpetrated by employees who recently underwent some kind of job change. Half of those had been fired, some had resigned, some were newly hired, and a few changed roles within the organization.*

The 'Wired' (2010) report quoted earlier shows that senior executives can also be specifically targeted because their access to information (if not to systems) is much greater. In this example the senior executive involved reacted sensibly. Socially, senior managers should have the highest degree of integration into the organization, and identification with its objectives. In some organizations, however, they come from an entrepreneurial background, which prides itself on cutting through obstacles, and may tend to regard themselves as above security procedures.

4.   Cleaners. Cleaners should not have system access, or access to sensitive information, but they do have considerable physical access to buildings. Cleaners are the most socially excluded of all employees. They often work alone, and do not even meet the people whose offices they clean after hours. They have no reason to identify with the organization where they are working, or its objectives. Typically, they are not well paid, come from marginalized elements of society, and may be vulnerable to inducements or pressures to perform simple and apparently innocuous tasks, e.g., to leave a few USB sticks lying around, or to collect apparently harmless data (e.g., room and telephone numbers).

5.   Everyone else! Not only direct employees, but also contractors, customers, partners, suppliers, etc., may have useful information or a degree of access. In addition, some functions may be outsourced, e.g., to call centres, software houses, etc., which may be outside the home country of an organization.

Most organizations introduce IT security policies. But these are often highly formal and subject to a review process. For example, BSI 27001 (BSI 2005, section 8.3) says:

The documented procedure for preventive action shall define requirements for:

(a) identifying potential nonconformities and their causes;
(b) evaluating the need for action to prevent occurrence of nonconformities;
(c) determining and implementing preventive action needed;
(d) recording results of action taken (see 4.3.3); and
(e) reviewing of preventive action taken.

The organization shall identify changed risks and identify preventive action requirements focusing attention on significantly changed risks.

On training, BSI 27001 (BSI 2005, section 5.2.2) states:

The organization shall ensure that all personnel who are assigned responsibilities defined in the ISMS are competent to perform the required tasks by:

- *determining the necessary competencies for personnel performing work effecting the ISMS;*
- *providing training or taking other actions (e.g. employing competent personnel) to satisfy these needs;*
- *evaluating the effectiveness of the actions taken; and*
- *maintaining records of education, training, skills, experience and qualifications (see 4.3.3).*

The organization shall also ensure that all relevant personnel are aware of the relevance and importance of their information security activities and how they contribute to the achievement of the ISMS objectives.

How practical this is, particularly for small and medium sized enterprises (SMEs), is another matter. At worst, highly formalized bureaucratic procedures may lead to a kind of 'paper safety', in which audit reports show satisfactory performance, but employees are tacitly aware of 'short cuts' and failings.

2.5   The Contrast with the Real World

On the one hand, businesses try to be efficient, responsive, and to satisfy customer needs. On the other, they introduce security policies that may make work more difficult, more time-consuming and more frustrating for employees.

Harley (1998: 23) cites the example of password changes:

> *It's accepted that frequent password changes make it harder for an intruder to guess a given user's password. However, they also make it harder for the user to remember his/her password. He/she is thus encouraged to attempt subversive strategies such as:*
>
> - *changing a password by some easily guessed technique such as adding 1, 2, 3 etc. to the password they had before the latest enforced change.*
> - *changing a password several times in succession so that the password history expires, allowing them to revert to a previously held password.*
> - *using the same password on several systems and changing them all at the same time so as to cut down on the number of passwords they need to remember.*
> - *aides-memoire such as PostIts, notes in the purse, wallet or personal organizer, biro on the back of the wrist ...*
>
> *How much data is there which 'validates' 'known truths' like 'frequent password changes make it harder for an intruder to guess a given user's password'? Do we need to examine such 'received wisdom' more closely?*

Passwords are only one example. There will always be a trade-off between efficiency and security, and between security and 'user-friendliness' (which is essential in dealing with human beings). Another example comes from a pseudonymous article in *Phrack* (2008) magazine, discussing an attack on the Australian Department of Defence, which says:

> *One of the fundamental problems with making rules is the existence of anomalous circumstances – exceptions – which most of us are aware of;) ... Creating a criteria and then an implementation procedure for security devices takes a long time, it is also expensive for the company doing the implementation – as they must pay for the DSD staff's time to do criteria evaluations – for their specific implementation of their product ... These rules are followed stringently at the time of a particular installation ... The amount of beaurecracy [sic] found in the*

DSD is mind-blowing. Thus their ability to move quickly on any given specific flaw in security is AT TIMES small.

In other words, tight security polices can slow down an organization's reactions to an attack, and in an attempt to be comprehensive, can also overlook 'anomalous circumstances'.

Harley (1998: 11) lists 'seven deadly vices' in system users, which together lead to many security breaches. These are:

1. Gullibility: believing a hard luck story from a caller;

2. Curiosity: opening an attachment because it looks interesting;

3. Courtesy: genuinely wanting to help a caller;

4. Greed: hoping to get something for nothing, e.g., download free software;

5. Diffidence: not wanting to confront the CEO when she is not wearing her security pass;

6. Thoughtlessness;

7. Apathy (Q: Which is the most useful to a social engineer? Ignorance or apathy? A: I don't know and I don't care);

To this list, we would add:

8. Misplaced 'common sense': recognising that sometimes organizational effectiveness requires short-cuts, but being unlucky enough to recognize this at the wrong time.

Many of these 'vices' are, in other contexts, virtues. Curiosity, courtesy, diffidence, etc., are socially important. Receptionists and switchboard staff cannot be trained to be courteous and helpful, and at the same time to be suspicious and to give nothing away.

Sales staff are trained to listen and respond to potential customers, not to be suspicious of them and question their motives. Sometimes new employees are put into front-line situations before they have had time to complete (and to assimilate) their full security training. Sometimes security training is too expensive and takes too long: companies cannot afford as much as they would like. 'Common sense' is something most of us use from time to time when we ignore or bypass a security rule that gets in the way in a situation, which is obviously (to us at least) 'safe'.

Examples seen by the author 'in the wild' include:

1.   Access granted to a secure building which normally requires a photo-ID. The visitor had forgotten his photo-id, but was 'recognized' by an employee of the organization who expected him, but had never actually met him.

2.   Switchboard operators giving out information about senior staff travel plans to callers. (The company involved makes a point of not naming its senior staff on its website; however they are all members of LinkedIn. Ringing up and asking to speak to the MD by name led the operator to assume that the caller was a friend.)

3.   Security staff obliged to insist that visitors enter via a security gate, even though there was no fence next to it (the fence had not yet been installed, the gate stood alone!)

None of these examples led to security problems. In each case, the request was genuine and the employee acted with 'common sense' to balance the security procedures against the needs of the business of the day.

It is tempting to try to construct sets of rules and procedures (reinforced by software and hardware systems) to ensure that every possible breach is covered off. But, as Harley (1998) implies and *Phrack* (2008) demonstrates, sometimes the stricter systems are counter-productive. Not only do they slow the business down, but they lead to staff finding 'workarounds' which are in themselves insecure. The key is to develop judgement, as well as rules and procedures.

2.6   Conclusion

Harley (1998: 9) advocates:

> *countering malicious social engineering with constructive social engineering through education. Whereas the Social Engineer will want*

to exploit the victim's behaviour without necessarily modifying it, the aware security professional will be more concerned with the behaviour modification involved in the education of the security-unaware user.

This book and the 'Alternative Worlds' project, is dedicated to this objective – better security education. The authors of this book believe that this must be different to, and more radical in its approach, than conventional security training. We believe it provides a better training interface – 'constructive social engineering', to use Harley's (1998) term, for trainees. It will improve organizational learning by developing judgement, exposing staff to simulated attacks in a safe environment. Training is aimed at developing judgement, rather than giving factual instructions. (For instance, the only answer to 'should I give this caller the e-mail address of the CEO?' is that it depends on the circumstances.)

The 'Alternative Worlds' system is based around a series of 'issues'. Examples might be:

- how to handle inquisitive callers;

- what to do with suspect e-mails or USB sticks; and

- what to do if your computer appears to be having problems.

The system contains several sets of scenarios. Each scenario raises the issues you have defined, but against a different background. The correct answer may be different in each scenario, but in considering the background and selecting an answer, the trainee is developing the sort of judgement you need him or her to exhibit. After working through several scenarios, the user builds up a profile on several pre-defined axes, based on the answers he or she chose. This provides an overall score, gives an indication of which areas he or she needs to improve, and can include links to advice or material about these areas.

The pre-defined 'axes' align with difficult choices. For instance, is the user too courteous or too diffident? Are they too curious, or not curious enough? They also test for knowledge, e.g., whether a particular action is against the organization's policies. Later, these can be developed into full-blown 'exercise' scenarios where groups can work though the effect of a major attack. The data collection exercises organized through the research workshops enabled questions to be posed, additional questions that users might face to be identified, and judgements made regarding correct responses.

References

Note: references are deliberately not given for some of the 'hacking tools' alluded to in the text. Please be aware that, in some cases, following up internet links offering these tools may lead to your own systems becoming infected. These links are a good example of 'social engineering'!

BSI. 2005. Information Technology – Security Techniques — Information Security Management Systems – Requirements. British Standards Institute BS ISO/IEC 27001:2005. London: BSI.

Cialdini, R. 1993. *Influence, the Psychology of Persuasion*. New York, NY: Quill.

CNET. 2003. 'Slammer' attacks may become way of life for Net: By R. Lemos, Staff Writer, CNET News.com. Available at: http://news.cnet.com/2009-1001-983540.html [accessed: 6 February 2010].

ComputerWorld. 2010. Available at: http://www.computerworlduk.com/news/security/20048/pwc-cost-of-security-breaches-triples-in-two-years-for-uk-firms/.

CDC. 2010. Cult of the Dead Cow website. Available at: http://w3.cultdeadcow.com/cms/about.html.

Davis, B.J. 2007. Situational prevention and penetration testing: A proactive approach to social engineering in organizations, in *Terrorism Issues: Threat Assessment, Consequences and Prevention*, edited by A.W. Merkidze. New York, NY: Nova Science Publishers, Inc., 175–88.

Dynes, S. et al. 2006. Costs to the U.S. economy of information infrastructure failures: Estimates from field studies and economic data. Proceedings of the Fifth Workshop on the Economics of Information Security (Cambridge: Cambridge University). Available at: http://www.ists.dartmouth.edu/library/207.pdf

El Pais. 2010. El ordenador de Spanair que anotaba los fallos en los aviones tenía virus: La computadora no operaba correctamente por unos programas 'troyanos' JOSÉ ANTONIO HERNÁNDEZ, Madrid. Available at: http://www.elpais.com/articulo/espana/ordenador/Spanair/anotaba/fallos/aviones/tenia/virus/elpepiesp/20100820elpepinac_11/Tes [accessed: 20 August 2010].

Guardian, The. 2010. Afghanistan: The war logs. Blog posting (no date). Available at http://www.guardian.co.uk/world/datablog/2010/jul/25/wikileaks-afghanistan-data.

Harley, D. 1998. Re-floating the Titanic: Dealing with Social Engineering Attacks. Presented at EICAR 1998. London: Imperial Cancer Research Fund. Available at http://smallbluegreenblog.files.wordpress.com/2010/04/eicar98.pdf.

Immunity. (2010). Website. Available at: http://www.immunityinc.com/products-immdbg.shtml [accessed: October, 2010].

Mitnick, K. 2002. *The Art of Deception*. Indianapolis, IN: Wiley Publishing Ltd.

Pagnamenta, R. 2010. Shell investigates posting of personal data, *The Times*, 13 February 2010). Available at: http://business.timesonline.co.uk/tol/business/industry_sectors/natural_resources/article7025711.ece.

Phrack. 2008. The Finn: Australian Restricted Defense Networks and FISSO Issue 65. Available at: http://phrack.org/issues.html?issue=65&id=9#article.

PwC. 2010a. PricewaterhouseCoopers, Information Security Breaches Survey 2010. Available at: http://www.pwc.co.uk/pdf/premium/isbs_survey_2010_executive_summary.pdf and http://www.pwc.co.uk/pdf/premium/isbs_survey_2010_technical_report.pdf.

PwC. 2010b. Press release by PricewaterhouseCoopers, 28 April 2010. Available at: http://www.ukmediacentre.pwc.com/News-Releases/New-wave-of-security-breaches-hitting-UK-businesses-costing-thcm-billions-new-report-shows-e8d.aspx.

Rahman, H.A., Beznosov, K. and Martí, J.R. 2009. Identification of sources of failures and their propagation in critical infrastructures from 12 years of public failure reports, *International Journal of Critical Infrastructures*, 5(3). Available at: http://lersse-dl.ece.ubc.ca/record/181/files/181.pdf.

Register. 2009. Conficker left Manchester unable to issue traffic tickets: Infection cost £1.5m in total. By J. Leyden, 1 July 2009. Available at: http://www.theregister.co.uk/2009/07/01/conficker_council_infection/.

Reuters. 2010. Spanish 'botnet' potent enough to attack country: Police. Report by T. Larraz, Madrid, 3 March 2010. Available at: http://www.reuters.com/article/idUSTRE6214ST20100303.

SIFY. 2010. DTH customers hit by Insat-4B power glitch. Available at: http://sify.com/finance/dth-customers-hit-by-insat-4b-power-glitch-news-default-khjxObcfghg.html [accessed: 7 September 2010].

Slade, G. 2010. Deniability tools are essential to strong privacy. StegoStik Limited. Available at: www.stegostik.co.uk.

Verizon. 2010. Data Breach Investigations Report. Available at http://www.verizonbusiness.com/resources/reports/rp_2010-data-breach-report_en_xg.pdf.

Whitaker, A., Evans, K. and Voth, J.B. 2009. *Chained Exploits*. Boston, MA: Pearson Education.

Wikipedia. 2010a. Article on Social Engineering. Available at: http://en.wikipedia.org/wiki/Social_engineering_(security) [accessed: October, 2010].

Wikipedia. 2010b. Article on Adrian Lamo. Available at: http://en.wikipedia.org/wiki/Adrian_lamo [accessed: October, 2010].

Wikipedia. 2010c. Article on the Yes Men. Available at: http://en.wikipedia.org/
    wiki/Yes_men [accessed: October, 2010].
Wikipedia. 2010d. Article on Chaos Computer Club. Available at: http://
    en.wikipedia.org/wiki/Chaos_Computer_Club [accessed: October, 2010].
Wikipedia. 2010e. Article on Phrack. Available at: http://en.wikipedia.org/wiki/
    Phrack [accessed: October, 2010].
Wikipedia. 2010f. Article on 2600. Available at: http://en.wikipedia.org/
    wiki/2600:_The_Hacker_Quarterly [accessed: October, 2010].
Wired. 2002. Michael Kaplan 'Three blind freaks', February 2004. Available at:
    http://www.wired.com/wired/archive/12.02/phreaks.html.
Wired. 2010. Kim Zetter, 'Hackers Targeted Oil Companies for Oil-Location
    Data', 26 January. Available at: http://www.wired.com/threatlevel/2010/01/
    hack-for-oil/.
ZDNet. 2003. Matt Loney, 'SQL Slammer worm wreaks havoc on Internet',
    ZDNet.co.uk, 26 January. Available at: http://www.zdnet.co.uk/news/
    security-management/2003/01/26/sql-slammer-worm-wreaks-havoc-on-
    internet-2129330/.
Zone-h. 2010. Kevin Fernandez, Twitter and Baidu hijacked by 'Iranian Cyber
    Army', Available at: http://www.zone-h.org/news/id/4733 [accessed: 13
    January 2010].

3

Organizational Issues Relating to Critical Information Infrastructure Protection

3.0 Introduction

It can be suggested that information breaches highlight the fact that inadequate security systems and procedures are in place within an organization and also, the expertise and commitment of those undertaking such activities is increasing. Employees should guard against providing critical information to strangers and need to be kept informed about the consequences associated with data and information leakages. Governments around the world have become concerned at the increasing number and sophistication of malware that is available and the speed at which it is produced and enters the network. Added to this is the prospect of denial of service attacks and the fact that domestic intelligence, law enforcement and security agencies will, it can be assumed, need to work more closely with their counterparts in other parts of the world if, that is, they are to disrupt and curtail the actions of organized criminal syndicates. Owing to the fact that new technologies are emerging, it can be assumed that organized criminal syndicates and various cyber criminals will continue to identify weaknesses, which they aim to exploit and turn to their advantage.

One of the issues confronting security specialists and government advisors, is that often IT managers in affected organizations react too slowly to an attack or staff do not want to make public the fact that they have not implemented a solution quickly enough. A key issue is how company staff update themselves in order to respond more quickly to an attack. Also, what resources should be put into training and staff development in order to ensure that staff are well able to counter attacks when they occur? Various metrics have been proposed that can assist IT managers to prepare their staff for a number of attacks. For example, Skybox are involved in firewall assurance and examine the settings of firewalls and alert IT managers about mis-configurations and how to optimize firewall configurations; and their approach to network assurance involves mapping and analysis that is aimed at reducing network configuration exposure (see http://www.skyboxsecurity.com/sites/default/files/CaseStudy_Actionable RiskMetricsFISMAAutomation_August2010.pdf [accessed: 24 November 2010]).

A distinction can be made between data that is of a sensitive or confidential nature and data that is general or in the public domain. What can be noted is that issues of privacy are paramount and that society has an expectation that data will be safeguarded and if it is traded, those that have provided the data/ information will be consulted beforehand. But this is not always the case and when data/information breaches occur, the publicity surrounding the event is quite forceful and the matter intensifies if an official inquiry is undertaken to look more deeply into the matter. Having said this, it can be acknowledged that most cyber attacks involve data that is valuable and an individual's right to privacy is secondary.

Large data sets are much more commonly used by government now. Data is sometimes placed with third parties that either may not understand why they should keep the data as secure as they should or are reluctant to invest in extensive security procedures to ensure that it is in fact held securely. When data breaches or losses occur, the ramifications can be serious and the ripples of discontent can linger for some time, especially if the media looks more deeply into the situation.

During the 2010 St George's House Annual Lecture, Lord Winston (2011: 11), provided a number of insights and recommendations in his talked entitled 'Scientists & Citizens':

> In being more science-literate, we might consider that the announcement of a new discovery is almost is heralded by exaggerated claims for its immediate value, that many technological advances have a threatening aspect which is not usually recognised at the time of the invention, that most human advances have beneficial applications which are not envisaged when the discovery is first made and that many really important discoveries are arrived at by serendipity.

> Communication is a two-way process. Good engagement with the public involves not merely imparting information, but listening to and responding to the ideas, questions, and concerns of the public ...

We should consider the ethical problems raised by the application of our work ...

Commercial interests so often promoted by governments and universities cannot be disregarded if technology is to be exploited for public good. But scientists need to be aware of the dangers of conflicts of interest. The history of science shows that the pursuit of commercial interests can lead to the loss of public confidence.

Although data may be viewed as a commodity to be traded, what needs to be pointed out is that there are technical, legal and ethical issues associated with data and information being misused, and although more control may be advocated, what is needed is a greater awareness of how individuals perceive the risks associated with making data (especially sensitive or personal data) available in the first place.

This chapter addresses a number of issues. Placing critical information infrastructure protection in context (Section 3.1) is followed by current issues, threats and ways to co-operate (Section 3.2). Reference is made to a joint training approach (Section 3.3) and then attention is given to organizational culture and corporate security education (Section 3.4). A joint security approach is highlighted (Section 3.5) and key aspects relating to disaster and emergency management are discussed (Section 3.6). The case for developing a joint security approach is made (Section 3.7 and this is followed by information relating to a new stakeholder security agenda (Section 3.8). Attention is given to cyber security and an organizational response (Section 3.9) and this is followed by a conclusion (Section 3.10).

3.1   Placing Critical Information Infrastructure Protection in Context

Organizations all over the world are highly dependent on information technology and as a result need to ensure that the increasing number of cyber threats, are dealt with in a constructive and timely manner. Electronic communication services and networks provide the backbone of the European economy and are vital to citizens, businesses and governments. Critical Information Infrastructure Protection (CIIP) is a vital component of national security and as such requires that policy makers and their advisors, place Critical Information Infrastructure Protection, not in a national context, but a global context.

It is a well-known fact that most Western European countries have established sophisticated and comprehensive CIIP organizations and systems, involving governmental agencies from different ministries, with a variety of current and future oriented initiatives. In the UK, the Centre for the Protection of National Infrastructure (CPNI), has done much to promote information security awareness and its staff work closely with senior managers and industry representatives to ensure that they can avail themselves of the information security knowledge that is available. CPNI also works closely with the European Network and Information Security Agency (ENISA). Both CPNI and ENISA provide advice and guidance with respect to security breaches and how to rectify them using specific information security tools. Both organizations stress the fact that managers need to be aware of current and evolving technological oriented security risks and also the problems and issues associated with human behaviour that could undermine an organization's position. The main focus of the work is to ensure that good practice is nurtured and shared, and as a consequence, organizations are better protected against a range of threats.

Across the Atlantic, the United States Computer Emergency Readiness Team (US-Cert):

> is charged with providing response support and defense against cyber attacks for the Federal Civil Executive Branch (.gov) and information sharing and collaboration with state and local government, industry and international partners.

> US-CERT interacts with federal agencies, industry, the research community, state and local governments, and others to disseminate reasoned and actionable cyber security information to the public.

> Information is available from the US-CERT web site, mailing lists, and RSS channels.

> US-CERT also provides a way for citizens, businesses, and other institutions to communicate and coordinate directly with the United States government about cyber security (see http://www.us-cert.gov/aboutus.html [accessed: 23 November 2010]).

These organizations try to cover all the different facets of CIIP, ranging from reducing vulnerabilities and fighting computer crime to building up defences against cyber terrorism. It is worth bearing in mind the fact that as well as protecting Critical National Infrastructure, governments and law enforcement officers in particular, need to be aware of and actively involved in a multitude of tasks that are aimed at eradicating or disrupting those involved in counterfeiting, drug and human trafficking, money laundering, motor industry theft, identity theft, and establishing terrorism networks. Cyber security covers all sorts of threats and is on the agenda of most governments of developed economies. What can be ascertained also, is that the business and security management models that are in place, need to be adapted in order to provide a robust counter-threat strategy that is sustainable through time and which raises the profile of corporate security staff. In the past, different issues have been handled by different regulations or company departments (e.g., health and safety, IT, financial compliance). IT systems and their attractiveness transcend these silos, and it is increasingly necessary for those responding to them to work together.

3.2   Current Issues, Threats and Ways to Co-operate

Evidence from the US puts into perspective the problems that President Obama's Administration is currently facing with respect to cyber security breaches (Lovely 2010):

> *Congress and other government agencies are under a cyber attack an average of 1.8 billion times a month, a number that has been growing exponentially since President Barack Obama took office.*

> *In 2008, security events caused by vectors including worms, Trojan horses and spybots averaged 8 million hits per month. That number skyrocketed to 1.6 billion in 2009 and climbed to 1.8 billion this year, according to Senate Sergeant-at-Arms Terrance Gainer.*

> *The Senate Security Operations Center alone receives 13.9 million of those attempts per day.*

> *'We operate in an escalating attack environment in which threats to our information infrastructure are increasing in both frequency and sophistication', Gainer wrote in testimony submitted to a Senate Appropriations subcommittee last night. 'Our raw numbers bear this out, so we must remain on guard'.*

The vast majority of the attacks have been stopped by the network's automated system defenses, but cyber attackers have become smarter.

Attacks are increasingly focused on infiltrating application software on Hill staffer computers, including Adobe Acrobat, Microsoft Office and Internet Explorer, which may not have the latest security patches.

Attackers have originated from both domestic and numerous foreign sources, and some have caused noticeable problems.

In the last five months of 2009, 87 Senate offices, 13 Senate committees and seven other offices were attacked by spear-phishing attacks, which appeared as e-mail messages to staffers, urging them to open infected attachments or click on bad links.

Malicious content was successfully delivered to Senate computers approximately four times each month.

Offices and committees were attacked an average of 18 times per month.

Last night during an Appropriations subcommittee budget hearing, Gainer asked Chairman Ben Nelson (D-Neb.) and ranking member Lisa Murkowski to allot $1 million for information technology consulting and equipment within the total budget request of $239 million.

Recent infections have been especially hard for his office to detect, Gainer said.

'I don't think there will ever be an end in sight. The amount of people trying to get at us is increasing', Gainer told Nelson, when Nelson asked whether Congress's computer systems were close to being fully protected.

'I think we're very safe', said Gainer. 'It's a continued and constant threat. Our adversaries are getting sharper, and we have to be sharper'.

Referring to the cyber attacks that were unleashed on Estonia over a period of two weeks in April/May 2007, Brenner (2009: 1–12) is clear that botnets have been used to attack other countries, to cripple a country's infrastructure, and to paralyze the government and the economy (Brenner 2009: 65). Such attacks can be mounted without the attackers even being identified, and certainly without any possibility of them being apprehended, whether they are mounted by governments, criminals or activists.

Institutions such as INTERPOL and EUROPOL have, according to Watson (2005), done much to facilitate information and teamwork among European law enforcement officers and it is pleasing to report that over the years both these organizations have had noticeable successes with respect to drug enforcement and thwarting terrorist actions, and undertaking initiatives to facilitate co-operation between EU states, the US and the Russian Federation. Watson (2005) has provided highly relevant insights into future security and intelligence policy by stating that:

> The creation of Europol can be seen as a unique milestone in the creation of international policing bodies. This is due, in part, to its close association with the European integration process, and the fact that its origins are political, as opposed to functional. Indeed, unlike which was established in order to facilitate the sharing of information between states – an obvious need, Europol can claim no such immediate legitimacy. However, although it may be true that to begin with, law enforcement within the EU had not demanded the establishment of such a body, it has still managed to grow and increase its remit. Further, in association with other EU bodies, including EuroJust, Europol has managed to calve a distinct and increasingly relevant 'niche' in the policing field.

ENISA are engaged in a wide range of activities ranging from organizing conferences on specific themes to producing well-defined training material. ENISA has produced a range of training material for managers in small- and medium-sized enterprises that focus attention on raising awareness among employees relating to e-mail security, malicious software, identity theft prevention, use of the internet at home, security while travelling and also when working remotely (see http://www.enisa.europa.eu/act/ar/deliverables [accessed: 23 November 2010]). In 2010, ENISA conducted the first Pan-European Cyber Security Exercise that was in effect a 'cyber stress test' for Europe, aimed at testing Europe's readiness to deal with online threats made against critical infrastructure. It involved 33 European countries, 22 of which actively participated in the scenario, and eight observers and a large number of specialists and experts were also involved (see http://www.enisa.europa. eu/media/press-releases/cyber-europe-2010-a-successful-2019cyber-stress-test2019-for-europe [accessed: 23 November 2010]).

There can be no doubt that governments will in the future need to pay more attention to preventing cyber disruptions of various kinds. For example, organized criminal syndicates and terrorist networks are keen to embrace technology for their own means and are known to recruit highly gifted young people with computer skills. In order to fully understand the ramifications of this, it is essential that those possessing expertise and knowledge make themselves available to assist law enforcement, intelligence and security personnel in their duties. It can also be suggested that there needs to be better co-operation between government bodies, industry and academia with respect to identifying knowledge and skill gaps, and putting in place a range of information assurance and information security courses and programmes that help address these issues and which also raise awareness and stimulate research into cyber security more generally. Drawing on the academic literature, it is possible to suggest that a joint approach (Trim and Lee 2006: 151) to counteract cyber threats is appropriate in the sense that by drawing on existing knowledge, and developing harmonious working relationships with partner organizations that result in mutuality, senior managers can adopt a sensitive leadership style, which ensures that those involved in solving problems do so by discussing them in an open and proactive manner. This being the case, a joint decision-making process can be adopted that has a human-centric approach to security (Jones and Trim 2009: 166). For example, while at work, people engage in certain activities that may put the organization they work for at risk. This is done knowingly or in innocence and can result in a vulnerability being exploited in one of several ways. Hence, whatever security measures are put in place, they must be aligned with or take into account human behaviour and how human behaviour changes through time. It may be, for example, that government and industry work together in order to ensure that technology and the application of technology does not put organizations at risk. Countermeasures need to be put in place that are judged to be adequate and robust enough during an externally orchestrated or internally orchestrated attack.

Infrastructures create interdependencies (Johnson and Williams 2008: 5) and it is these interdependencies that policy makers and their advisors need to recognize as being weak links in the Critical Information Infrastructure (CII) chain. Bearing this in mind, it can be suggested that a human-centric approach to security is well founded (support is gaining ground from intelligence and security experts) and that the call for greater co-operation between the private and public sectors (Jones and Trim 2009: 167) is well founded. Further support for enhanced co-operation in the form of a logical argument is provided by Jones and Trim (2009: 167):

> *A range of threat 'vectors' such as physical and cyber attack has led large corporations to examine the relationship between their security strategy and the risk oriented contingency plans of the various components of the organisation.*

However, change will not happen just because it is considered necessary – the process of change needs to be managed. Arguments need to be put forward to stimulate new approaches/methods of solving current and evolving problems. For example, situated learning, which stresses authentic and real-world contexts; and social interaction, characterized by people working 'together in a situated activity to construct shared understandings', are deemed relevant as regards the development of an individual's knowledge base (Krajcik and Blumenfeld 2009: 319). Another important approach to learning is the use of co-operation. Collins (2009: 53) indicates that people can be made to work in pairs in order to solve problems, and this suggests that teamwork is deemed useful with respect to identifying solutions for complex problems.

3.3   A Joint Training Approach

Various experts have over the years suggested that a more focused approach needs to be taken to training law enforcement, intelligence and security staff, and should this indeed be the case, a more robust cyber security skill base will be created. Research is needed to understand the psychological and social factors behind cyber security crimes. The findings can be made public at best practice seminars and the accumulated expertise should manifest in more strict law enforcement policies being implemented and/or a better understanding of how the problem can be tackled. The years ahead are likely to witness greater co-operation in counteracting illegal cross-border activity (both physical and electronic), however, the solutions are less likely to emanate from one place only. With respect to the issue of cyber security, it is interesting to note that although the International Standard for Information Security Management, ISO 27001 states what the standard is, it 'does not provide detailed guidance on how it should be implemented in any particular organisation' (Jones and Trim 2009: 169). This may suggest that more needs to be done or, possibly, the lead has to come more directly from the government. Indeed, the UK government has recognized that cyber space represents a double-bladed sword:

> *Cyber security embraces both the protection of UK interests in cyber space and also the pursuit of wider UK security policy through exploitation of the many opportunities that cyber space offers (Cabinet Office 2009: 9).*

Referring to a joint approach to training, what needs to be acknowledged is that inter-organizational and intra-organizational factors and considerations need to influence the way that knowledge is developed and shared between partner organizations, and also, how experience gained can result in better decisions being made and turned into policy and strategy. For example, the term mutuality can be viewed from the perspective of people benefiting in some way from an activity or event. Those that benefit may be employed by the same organization but are based in different departments or work for different organizations and possess different specialisms. What can be acknowledged is that they will share a common aim/objective, and will work together in order to make more informed decisions. Exchanging ideas and experiences, and thus reaching agreement with respect to what vulnerabilities exist and those that are perceived as evolving, should allow people to develop a common understanding that manifests in better planning and risk mitigation. The complexity of this needs to be appreciated owing to the fact that power relations, trust and risk, structures and mechanisms, and social ties are all deemed important factors with respect to understanding what inter-organizational knowledge transfer involves (Easterby-Smith et al. 2008: 679). These factors and indeed others, are influential in developing certain types of trust based relationships between people based in different departments/functions, and in different organizations that operate in different parts of the world.

3.4   Organizational Culture and Corporate Security Education

Much has been written about leadership within organizations and it is acknowledged that there are various leadership theories that embrace style and decision-making approaches, and place these within the context of a business model. Bass (1990: 21) has paid attention to this and states:

> *Superior leadership performance – transformational leadership – occurs when leaders broaden and elevate the interests of their employees, when*

*they generate awareness and acceptance of the purpose and mission of
the group, and when they stir their employees to look beyond their own
self-interest for the good of the group. Transformational leaders achieve
these results in one or more ways. They may be charismatic to their
followers and thus inspire them; they may meet the emotional needs
of each employee; and/or they may intellectually stimulate employees.*

A transformational leader places a high emphasis on trust and trust-based
relationships, and considers that employees need to be in harmony with the
organization's objectives. This can be interpreted as an individual employee
having the same value system as their peers (and other employees) and that
there is a match between the employee's value system and the organization's
value system, hence internal mutuality. According to Kakabadse (2000: 6), a
transformational leader is a good listener and has the confidence to empower
staff so that organizational change is accepted and progresses as planned.
However, it is recognized that a transformational leader needs to manage
all tasks adequately and maintain control at all times. Furthermore, senior
managers need to both embrace and remain committed to organizational
learning, if the organization is to develop a transformational leadership style.

It is necessary at this point to stop and reflect and to suggest that a
transactional leadership style, which is known to be hierarchical in orientation
and as Bratton et al. (2005: 216) state: 'rooted in the usual exchange of material
rewards for effort', may be appropriate when a specific type of business model
is in place and is relevant to the environment/industry setting. For example,
a transactional leadership style is possibly beneficial when the business
relationship is based on achieving immediate needs and both or all parties
consider that they gain from the relationship/transaction and deem it to be fair.
However, the relationship is not necessarily long term and can be considered
for the purpose and is exchange oriented.

In order that a transformational leadership style emerges, it is essential that
top management view change as incremental and adopt a proactive approach
to managing change. This demands that all the organizational members adhere
to the same organizational value system. An organization's cultural value
system will mutate through time and it is important to recognize this and to
put in place various management development support mechanisms that are
aimed at facilitating staff development. By viewing management development
from a theory building perspective, it is possible to define clearly what needs to
be done in order to develop the skill base of the employees and ensure that each

individual member of staff fulfils, within reason, their own career aspirations. An organization's set of values can be communicated through internal marketing and can be made known using sound public relations methods. It can also be suggested that Agency Theory is useful for concentrating attention on a broad range of issues encompassed by a relationship formed and developed between two people. Within Agency Theory there are two distinct schools of thought: the positive theory of agency (the company is a nexus of contracts) and the theory of principal and agent (focuses on how the principal design's the agent's reward structure) (Douma and Schreuder 1998: 100). The central point to note is that reward, however defined, can be used to motivate staff to achieve a goal or set of objectives, and can be linked to career progression. Planned career progression does incorporate training and staff development programmes, and successful candidates that rise through the organization's hierarchy will be assigned titles and roles of responsibility.

Tensions between these two management approaches are exacerbated by the conflicting needs of cyber security. In order to maintain security, a rigid set of rules and procedures are necessary, and often enforced by corporate and government IT systems. Rewards are defined by adherence to these rules (or more strictly, by lack of breaches). On the other hand, these rules often slow down and frustrate people who are trying to 'get things done', particularly if they are operating in news areas, or are introducing changes to products, business models, or relationships. In this context, rewards are defined by success, by new products, new models, and new relationships successfully built up.

The two approaches are contrary to each other, and anyone who has worked in industry is aware of uneasy compromises that are often made between security and 'getting things done'. As Argyris (1999: 56) says:

> In real life, most organisations exhibit powerful defensive routines ... [which are] ... any action or policy intended to prevent the players from experiencing embarrassment or threat, and does so in ways that make it difficult to identify and reduce the causes of the embarrassment or threat. Defensive routines are overprotective and anti-learning ...

The problem is striking a balance, and using Agency Theory to define an appropriate reward structure may not always be as useful as expected. There is an inevitable tension between what Argyris (1999) calls 'espoused theories' (that is what we are officially doing, or think we are doing) and 'theories in use' (that is what we are actually doing), to which cyber security is particularly vulnerable. The field is so complex, and changes so quickly, that it is very difficult to design a reward structure that both prevents unauthorised 'security breaches' and rewards sensible use of initiative.

Lee (2005) has advocated that organizational learning can be used to promote an organization's value system and thus facilitate incremental change, which has been identified as being important for managing organizational change and individual, behavioural change. Indeed, as regards the implementation of transformational change, Lee (Trim 2009: 95) states that:

> *senior managers need to distinguish between leadership and strategic leadership, and adopt a dual leadership approach, in order that junior managers can devise and implement new management models that result in improved decision-making processes. The main advantage of this approach is that it should result in more open communication and an acceptance of what is known as institutionalizing organizational learning, which can facilitate government to government co-operation; government to organization co-operation; and organization to organizational co-operation.*

Lee (Trim 2009: 95) has taken this view a step further by suggesting that:

> *In order that an organization improves its level of performance, it is necessary for top management to make strategic decisions that provide it with a clearly defined direction. By embracing the concept of organizational learning, top management can encourage staff to improve their knowledge and skill base through time. However, problems do occur and a major problem is how top managers can encourage their staff to learn on a continuing basis, and to co-operate with staff outside their immediate department. The learning process is not just about acquiring knowledge and skills, it is also about developing a vision that is based on understanding the values that are promoted by top management.*

With specific attention to partnership arrangements, it can be argued that the level of dependency between organizations in a successful partnership arrangement increases through time and as a consequence managers will be required to share information (Carlile 2004) on a frequent basis. Inkpen and Currall (2004: 594–5) are adamant that as the level of dependency increases between partner organizations, 'partner willingness to provide access to information is likely to increase, thus providing the foundation for partner learning'. If, however, a partnership is judged to be failing/not achieving the objectives set, the reverse may be true. In such a situation action may be taken to realign the priorities of the organizations in the partnership arrangement and this may be achieved through closer working arrangements and adherence to a continuous improvement programme. The aim of the continuous improvement programme is to change the method of working or introduce new working practices and possibly, in the case of a severe situation, characterized by the failing organization, a change in an organization's value system. What is clear is that training and tailor-made staff development programmes can help to eradicate organizational inadequacies, by means of upgrading the skill base of individuals.

3.5   A Joint Security Approach

Law enforcement, government security and intelligence officers, as well as corporate security officers, need to be aware of how to develop long-term mutually oriented partnership arrangements that are based on information sharing, if that is, they are to gain the trust of those that they work with. The UK's Centre for the Protection of National Infrastructure (CPNI) has developed a set of 'Information Exchanges' (IEs), covering a range of industry sectors. These are informal regular meetings of senior IT staff, and CPNI officials, on a confidential basis. Members exchange information about current threats, and perhaps more important still, develop networks with whom they can consult if they themselves fall victim to a major attack. To ensure confidentiality, and therefore that members can speak openly, membership of these networks is on a personal basis, not a company basis. This is an excellent model for joint action, which replicates and extends the existing informal networks between system administrators, which have often provided the backbone of real-life responses to cyber threats.

An earlier and less successful CPNI initiative relating to information sharing (see http://www.warp.gov.uk/warps-explained.html [accessed: 23 November 2010]) in a structured manner, was the formation of:

> WARPs (short for Warning, Advice, and Reporting Points) ... developed
> to provide a cost effective method to support defence against attacks.
> Their purpose is to provide a specific community with the capability to
> share security related information – both problems and solutions – and
> thereby to develop more secure and responsive environments.

- *The WARP operator uses a website, e-mail, telephone, SMS, and occasional meetings (where possible) to send a personalised service of warnings and advice to the members. This will be mainly IT security advice (because there's so much of it, and it changes so rapidly), but can include other material (other threats, e-crime, contingency planning etc) as well.*

- *The operator also taps into the knowledge of the members themselves to help out other members using a bulletin board, meetings etc.*

- *There will usually be between 20 and 100 members in each WARP, otherwise it can lose that personal touch, and they will belong to a community (small businesses, local government, service providers, interest groups, etc.).*

- *A WARP operator does not have to be a technical expert in IT security as their main role is to facilitate the exchange of security related information within the WARP community. This would require good communication and management skills.*

- *A successful WARP will build up enough trust to encourage members to share details about their own incidents and problems, anonymously if need be, for the benefit of the rest.*

- *WARPs are run on a 'not-for-profit' basis.*

3.6   Disaster and Emergency Management

One of the present authors, Upton (2009) has focused attention on various aspects of disaster and emergency management, and favours the systems management approach. Addressing the issue of how to make simulation exercises more efficient, Upton (2009: 210) asserts that prescription by governments, or the proliferation of rules and guidance, does not always produce effective training exercises: the 'bottom up' approach, in which companies systematize their own experience and training skills, and their ability to learn from experience, is an alternative method. Indeed, Upton (2009: 210) has developed a software package:

> *which starts from a series of factual inputs (descriptive list of stakeholders, locations involved, and possible incident and response*

scenarios) and then uses artificial intelligence to create individual
scenarios, down to and including detailed injects for roleplayers.

This system makes it easier, indeed mostly automatic, for users to store and benefit from experience. The software system is known as 'Alternative Worlds', and writes emergency response/crisis management/business continuity training exercises (CAMIS Newsletter 2010: 6–7). The software system makes exercises more consistent and easier to manage, and stores expertise, so that good training results can be achieved by people with little experience of writing exercises.

The software system can be applied to many sectors, e.g., critical information infrastructure, transport and defence, and helps to build better resilience, more cheaply. It uses web-based software to write exercises quickly and easily. They can be used in exactly the same way as traditionally 'hand-written' exercises: most participants will not realize the difference. Users do not need to introduce new systems or change their training methods.

Trim (2005a) has indicated that, because the international environment is becoming increasingly unpredictable, policy makers need to realize that the elimination of risk and the reduction of uncertainty requires a joint approach to security and intelligence work, which is supported by government-to-government 'direct action' and company-to-government 'indirect action'. However, with respect to cyber issues, it is companies and not governments that control what goes on and it has to be remembered that companies can stop the internet in an instance. In view of the fact that man-made disasters can have just as large a psychological impact as a major natural disaster, it is worth suggesting that people see matters in a certain light and develop a certain perception that places cyber security threats in the same category as a large and somewhat devastating natural disaster. The key point to note is that a man-made disaster is likely to result in a lack of confidence among the general public as people consider that they are not adequately protected. Feeling less safe than previously can have the effect of people being less economically active. This can have ramifications for the economy (people travel less and have a reduced social life for example).

Evidence of this comes in the form of the cost (lost lives, fatal injuries, devastation totalling billions of dollars for example) and the fact that in some countries it is the people that take responsibility for organizing relief work and not the government. (This can be interpreted from the stance that some countries are judged to have bad governments in place.) However, there are many issues outstanding relating to how prepared society is with respect to a disaster and the following example provided by Upton (2007: 83–4) brings home some very firm realities.

> *The explosions at a fuel depot in Buncefield in the UK in December 2005 led to one of the largest fires in Europe since the second World War. Luckily there were no serious casualties, but the incident caused massive smoke plumes and much chaos. John Prescott, the Deputy Prime Minister, was quick to assure the House of Commons that: 'I can tell the House that, only three months ago, the emergency services in Hertfordshire conducted a successful exercise, covering just such an eventuality as occurred yesterday' (Hansard 2005).*

However, when the author wrote to the Government Office for the South East to ask what this exercise was, the reply was:

> *The fire service has carried out numerous exercises at the Buncefield Site. The last exercise was on the 18th November 2005. It was a water mains test exercise with six fire appliances and six fire crews in attendance. One thing that came out of the exercise was that water access was not the best due to positioning of certain hydrants.*

Clearly, this was nowhere near the scale of the Buncefield 'eventuality'. Fire Service officers have since confirmed, in seminars attended by the co-researcher Upton, that they had only ever exercised a fire in a single tank, never in more than one, and certainly not in all of them.

The Health and Safety Executive (HSE 2006) later confirmed that:

> *The Buncefield incident on 11th December 2005 has demonstrated the capability of a very large hydrocarbon leak to create a massive explosion with a destructive power beyond the typical 'worst case' normally used for on- and off-site emergency planning purposes.*

3.7 Developing a Joint Security Approach

The points cited above make clear that people need to view risks more clearly. The Global Intelligence and Security Environmental Sustainability (GISES)

Model represents a conceptual framework, which can be used to focus the attention of policy makers and their advisors on ways in which to disrupt and destroy criminal-terrorist network arrangements (Trim 2005a, 2005b). The GISES model embraces the concept of knowledge management, proactive leadership, team working and the sharing of information. By adopting the GISES model, it should be possible for intelligence and security professionals to create greater linkage between the public and private sectors, and to ensure that managers recognize that corporate security involves far more than is the case at present and that the expertise of corporate security professionals is made fully available to those involved in business continuity planning.

Various other models exist such as the Anti-Terrorist Business-Politico (ATBP) model (Trim and Caravelli 2007), which can be used to focus the collaborative efforts of those involved in fighting terrorism (corporate security specialists included). The ATBP model can be viewed as a generic model that focuses inter-government decision-making and it can be used to formulate and implement action plans to deal with both a particular threat and the consequences and ramifications (after effects) of an event/incident (Trim 2009: 99). An environmental and infrastructural risk assessment (EIRA) model is an output of the ATBP model (Trim and Caravelli 2007: 149). The main objective of the EIRA model is to focus attention on counteracting the actions of terrorists and facilitating the co-ordination of security and intelligence activities with those of law enforcement personnel.

3.8   A New Stakeholder Security Agenda

Work undertaken by Stirling Reid Limited and Birkbeck, University of London, to date has examined Critical Information Infrastructure (CII) failures, and what can be done at a human and organizational level to respond to them. This research provides much of the basis of this book. The co-operation between a government (the Technology Strategy Board is a government funded agency), a university (Birkbeck) and an SME is itself a good example of the benefits of greater co-operation between different sectors.

Fuerth (2006) is right to highlight the fact that the ever-increasing unpredictability of threats is worrying. This is another reason why those involved in security and intelligence work look more closely at the issues linking risk assessment, governance and compliance for example. Trim and Caravelli (2007: 5) have tried to add to the existing body of knowledge by stating that:

Risk is a broad based term that is often applied in various contexts and settings. The term risk is often linked with probability theory and this means that risk can be interpreted in a quantifiable manner. Experts involved in security and intelligence work are aware of the different definitions of risk that exist and make objective risk assessments that support policy decisions. The study of risk, uncertainty and vulnerability is therefore complicated and not as clear cut as one would expect. Issues such as psychological risk are difficult to quantify and need possibly to be associated with inner feelings of confidence, emotion and the 'feel good factor'. Furthermore, one needs to distinguish clearly between natural disasters and manmade disasters, if that is an objective analysis of risk is to be made. Risk also needs to be viewed from the perspective of an individual, a group and a community, if that is, the term is to have meaning.

It can be suggested that the term security needs to be more widely interpreted and understood than is the case at present. For example, Denney (2005: 121) suggests that '"Security" is a problematic concept since it appears to have different meanings in different contexts'. This may to some degree be related to the fact that the word security is interpreted in different ways. For example, the head of security in a company may deal with issues relating to information technology and the physical manning of the buildings/laboratories that are owned and occupied by company personnel. Those working for government and advising government may consider issues of importance such as food availability and the supply of water (the role of supermarkets and water treatment plant operators), and military operations (direct action and peacekeeping), and strategic issues such as non-proliferation. Reflecting on the fact that safety and security cut across all industries (an offshore oil platform or a chemical plant can have a complete range of safety features, and an office building can have extensive modern security systems), experience shows that these fail from time to time: the Piper Alpha fire in 1988, for example. As regards the latter, the platform had a series of safety systems, but some were broken, some were switched off, and some proved to be inadequate. Hence there is a clear link between safety and security, and are of equal importance whether to be viewed from a public sector or private sector perspective. In German usage, for example, the word 'sicherheit' is used to mean both 'safety' and 'security'.

In order that a more holistic view of security can be adopted it is necessary for various intra-organizational forms of working to be devised (Trim 2005a). As a result, security will be viewed as being of fundamental concern and greater attention will be given to it at board room level. Trim et al. (2009) have recognized the fact that organizations are becoming increasingly interdependent and this does mean that the new business models that are evolving place organizational resilience and sustainability in a different context. Understanding the level and degree of connectivity of organizations is paramount if senior management are to fully understand the issues revolving around Critical Information Infrastructure Protection (CIIP). The SATELLITE (Strategic Corporate Intelligence and Transformational Marketing) model designs in security to the strategic management process (Trim 2004; Trim et al. 2009) and both outlines and specifies the work undertaken through the creation of a Corporate Intelligence Staff Support Group, a Strategic Marketing Staff Support Group, a Corporate Security Management Group, an Internet Marketing Group, a Relationship Marketing Advisory Group and a SATELLITE Advisory Group. The model is somewhat generic in form and can be used by senior managers to integrate corporate security activities with a broader range of other strategic and operational activities.

Elsa Lee (2009: 131) is right to point out that although government departments and agencies have publicized what future threats are likely to manifest, the private sector needs to be more aware of how government and various organizations can co-ordinate an overall response effort. This brings us back to the key point. Managers in the private sector need to be fully aware of the damage that potential attacks can have and also that the response and

Table 3.1   The key SLEPT decision areas relating to CIIP

SLEPT Characteristics	CIIP Interdependencies
Social	Varied and complex. Need: a varied communication strategy aimed at the local (community), regional, national and international levels.
Legal	Initiatives to protect society (general public), commerce and industry.
Economic	Trading is international, integrated and based on mutuality, hence the immediate areas of risk/vulnerability are supply chains and their associated relationships.
Political	Semi-closed, different forms of regulation required: Government intervention policy may be viewed as essential.
Technological	Pull and push factors are evident, and so too are multiple tiers: fast moving and changing in scope with a solutions orientation requirement.
Needed outcomes Reasons for government intervention	To maintain the stability of society. To ensure that the quality of life is improved through time. To ensure that commerce and industry are sustainable and competitive. To counteract and prevent the actions of activists, organized criminals and terrorist networks. To ensure that overseas investors remain confident and invest in the country.

recovery plans in place need to be realistically defined. The Key SLEPT Decision Areas Relating to CIIP are highlighted in Table 3.1. If an adequate cyber security strategy is to be formulated and implemented, it is essential for top management to invest in robust countermeasures. An organization's response to a cyber attack has to be co-ordinated internally and, when necessary, information shared with government representatives so that government can be better informed about providing leadership as regards cyber defence. This should also have the desired effect of placing a nation's cyber security strategy within an international setting as increasingly, sophisticated cyber attacks are being launched from transnational criminal syndicates. As regards the latter, it can be suggested that in the future, there will be increased co-ordination between government and industry.

3.9   Cyber Security and an Organizational Response

Trim and Upton (2010a, 2010b) have made a number of observations as regards cyber security and the response that is needed. They are clear that, viewed holistically, Critical Information Infrastructure Protection interdependencies are providing both problems and opportunities. For example, they are keen to point out that senior managers may well be aware of the possible cyber threats but that they may not have established a suitable, well-developed response capacity. This must not be limited to precautionary measures such as firewalls for example. The sophistication and frequency of attacks means that some are likely to succeed, despite precautions. It is therefore essential to develop a response capacity, to limit the damage caused and to improve network security.

Taking into account the fact that the systems involved are extremely complex, and few people fully understand them all, it is not possible for managers and their support staff to have full knowledge of the situation and external assistance and advice is required, on an ongoing basis. This is particularly true of small companies that are in the growth phase of development. As with other types of security, there is a lot of judgement involved in striking a balance between security and risk appetite, and ultimately issues of cost become influential. And there is a permanent 'arms race': as the good guys close one loophole, the bad guys find another. In 2010, Microsoft issued a patch for a 17-year-old vulnerability that had only just been discovered (BBC News website 2010).

As we discuss later in this book, the reason why cyber attacks are growing exponentially is partly a technological one. Writing a good attack requires a minute inspection of many thousands of lines of 'assembly language' code, looking for vulnerabilities. Assembly language breaks down programming instructions to precise, step-by-step manipulation of a computer processor. As a result it is both complex and extremely verbose. Tools are now available to automate such searches, so that what might have taken a lonely anti-social hacker many hours of hard work, can now be done by a short program in a few minutes. These tools are very widely available – they are no longer the preserve of hacker websites but can be found in books from mainstream publishers (see, for example, Seitz 2009).

The cost of cyber attacks is causing increased concern among managers; for example, it is known that a lot of planning goes into preventing physical attacks on buildings. However, it is almost cost-free to make a security attack across the internet. Computer programs can be written to make thousands, even millions, of attacks, while their owners sleep. In many cases the owners are out of reach of national Police, or civil actions. They take few risks and they require little by way of technology or even knowledge. When you are being bombarded with cyber attacks in this way, it is highly likely that some will succeed. The most worrying aspects for managers is that a low probability, high impact attack will succeed, and the knock-on effects can be devastating.

Companies in traditional high-risk industries, such as the chemical industry, have emergency response procedures and teams to cope with the cases where something gets through the safety or security precautions. They train their response teams, and validate their plans, by emergency response exercises. Over time, the best of them develop an 'exercise culture', where their staff are used to exercises, take them seriously, and above all learn lessons from them and apply these lessons. In other cases, such as the Buncefield explosion at a fuel storage terminal in the UK in 2005, it is clear that the response plans were not adequate and that lessons had to be learned on the spot, at a high cost. What managers need to note from this is that the organization may face adverse publicity, which results in a fall in the share price and, ultimately, makes the organization vulnerable to a takeover. More importantly, however, people may die as a result of an explosion and this may have a devastating affect on a community in the same way as mining disasters have had in the past. If contamination results then obviously there may be severe environmental pollution that renders an area uninhabitable for many years. Again this can have a devastating effect on a community as schools may be closed and the population relocated to a safer area.

It has been reported that UK companies had fewer security breaches in 2008 compared with 2004, and this may be as a result of management putting a documented security policy in place, increasing the IT budget spent on security, providing ongoing security awareness training for staff, using strong (multi-factor) authentication, and implementing BS 7799/ISO 27001 (PricewaterhouseCoopers 2008: 2–3). On the other hand, it is clear that not all companies have full emergency response procedures for cyber attacks, and this is worrying bearing in mind the increasing intensity of cyber attacks.

UK companies have made progress in identifying key vulnerabilities and improving their security vis-à-vis backing up critical systems and data, deploying software that scans spyware, filtering incoming e-mail for spam, protecting websites with firewalls, scanning incoming e-mails for viruses, and encrypting wireless network transmissions (PricewaterhouseCoopers 2008: 2).

It is clear that the type, nature and intensity of threats will increase through time and cyber attacks in particular will be more deadly than first anticipated. It is unlikely that staff based in the IT department will be able to deal with the range of threats purely on their own, as some may involve insider assistance, and any serious threat will call for a wider concerted reaction by the company, for instance to the media in relation to ripples of discontent in the financial markets. For example, Smith (2010: 28) reported that criminal gangs, employing between 300 to 400 people, pretended to represent IT companies and fooled people into purchasing 'anti-virus' software costing £30, which then hacked into their computer records.

The threats that are manifesting are far more serious and organized criminal syndicates and hostile government agencies (carrying out acts of industrial espionage) are using a variety of techniques for their own ends. Individuals and organized criminal syndicates are turning to cyber crime because it is possible to make small investments and reap very large returns. So the economic justification is clear. As well as earning huge amounts of money from bogus 'anti-virus' software, criminal gangs are also reaping rewards from successful attacks on companies that result in ransom demands being met. Add to this the cost associated with disruption and the knock-on effects, it is not surprising to learn that the average cost of a worst incident in a year for a small company is thought to be between £10,000 and £20,000; and between £90,000 and £170,000 for a large company; and between £1 million and £2 million for a very large company (PricewaterhouseCoopers 2008: 2).

3.10   Conclusion

Safety incidents, security breaches or cyber attacks that have a great impact on an organization can challenge its sustainability. By having adequate security in place, it should be possible to utilize environmental scanning techniques to anticipate and predict a major event, and to possibly repulse it or limit the damage caused. In order to engage in effective environmental scanning, it is necessary that managers embrace business and competitive intelligence, and think strategically.

Putting procedures in place to handle incidents makes sense and training, in order to be effective, needs to be placed within the context of organizational learning. It is clear that exercising is one means of training for the unknown, which can improve awareness and create an opportunity for collective decision-making, in cases where the cause is probably unknown, and the full extent of the problem may not yet be known. It is doubly difficult to train for cyber emergencies, because so few people understand them, and because there is often very little to see while an attack is actually under way. Computer system logs are not very exciting. Neither is an empty bank account, or a foreign competitor who suddenly markets a copy of the organization's product, and gains rapid market share at the expense of the law-abiding company.

References

Argyris, C. 1999. *On Organisational Learning*. Malden, MA: Blackwell.

Bass, B.M. 1990. From transactional to transformational leadership: Learning to share the vision. *Organizational Dynamics*, (Winter), 19–31.

BBC News website. 2010. Microsoft to patch 17-year-old computer bug. Available at: http://news.bbc.co.uk/1/hi/8499859.stm [accessed: 5 February 2010].

Brenner, S.W. 2009. *Cyberthreats: The Emerging Fault Lines of the Nation State*. Oxford: Oxford University Press.

Bratton, J., Grint, K. and Nelson, D.L. 2005. *Organizational Leadership*. Mason, Ohio: South-Western/Thomson.

Cabinet Office. 2009. *Cyber Security Strategy of the United Kingdom: Safety, Security and Resilience in Cyber Space*. (Cm 7642, June). London: Cabinet Office.

CAMIS Newsletter (2010). Innovative emergency response simulation system research project: Stirling Reid Ltd and Birkbeck, 6 (1), 6–7.

Carlile, P.R. 2004. Transferring, translating, and transforming: An integrative framework for managing knowledge across boundaries. *Organization Science*, 15 (5), 555–68.

Collins, A. 2009. Cognitive apprenticeship, in *The Cambridge Handbook of the Learning Sciences*, edited by R.K. Sawyer. Cambridge: Cambridge University Press, 47–60.

Denney, D. 2005. *Risk and Society*. London: Sage Publications.

Douma, S. and Schreuder, H. 1998. *Economic Approaches to Organizations*. Hemel Hempstead: Prentice Hall Europe.

Easterby-Smith, M., Lyles, M.A. and Tsang, E.W.K. 2008. Inter-organizational knowledge transfer: Current themes and future prospects. *Journal of Management Studies*, 45 (4), 677–90.

Fuerth, L. 2006. Strategic myopia: The case for forward engagement. *The National Interest*, 83 (Spring), 58–63.

Hansard 2005. Monday 12 December at 3.32 pm: See Hansard record. Available at: http://www.parliament.the-stationery-office.co.uk/pa/cm200506/cm hansard/cm051212/debtext/51212-05.htm.

HSE. 2006. Health and Safety Executive: In a 'Safety Alert to operators of "COMAH" oil/fuel storage sites' sent out on 21 February 2006. Available at: http://www.hse.gov.uk/comah/buncefield/alert.htm.

Inkpen, A. and Currall, S. 2004. The coevolution of trust, control and learning in joint ventures. *Organization Science*, 15 (5), 586–99.

Kakabadse, A. 2000. From individual to team to cadre: Tracking leadership for the third millennium. *Strategic Change*, 9 (1) (January February), 5–16.

Krajcik, J.S. and Blumenfeld, P.C. 2009. Project based learning, in *The Cambridge Handbook of the Learning Sciences*, edited by R.K. Sawyer. Cambridge: Cambridge University Press, 317–33.

Jones, N. and Trim, P.R.J. 2009. Establishing a security culture: Pointers for senior management, in *Strategizing Resilience and Reducing Vulnerability*, edited by P.R.J. Trim and J. Caravelli. New York, NY: Nova Science Publishers, Inc., 165–79.

Johnson, C.W. and Williams, R. 2008. Computation support for identifying safety and security related dependencies between national critical infrastructures. Available at: http://www.dcs.gla.ac.uk/~johnson/papers/ IET_2008/National_Critical_InfrastructureFinal.pdf [accessed: 5 February 2010].

Lee, Y-I. 2005. A strategic model for facilitating inter-organizational and intra-organizational development. *The Second CAMIS Security Management Conference entitled Managing Complexity and Developing Partnership Initiatives*, Birkbeck College, University of London, 23 September.

Lee, E. 2009. *Homeland Security and Private Sector Business: Corporations' Role in Critical Infrastructure Protection*. Boca Raton, FL: CRC Press/Taylor & Francis Group.

Lovely, E. 2010. 'Cyberattacks explode in congress'. Available at: http://www.politico.com/news/stories/0310/33987.html [accessed: 17 March 2010].

PricewaterhouseCoopers. 2008. *2008 Information Security Breaches Survey: Technical Report*. London: Department for Business, Enterprise & Regulatory Reform.

Seitz, J. 2009. *Grey Hat Python: Python Programming for Hackers and Reverse Engineers*. San Francisco, CA: No Starch Press.

Smith, H. 2010. Crooks steal IDs in online 'security' con. *METRO*, 15 November, 28.

Trim, P.R.J. 2004. The strategic corporate intelligence and transformational marketing (SATELLITE) model. *Marketing Intelligence and Planning*, 22 (2), 240–56.

Trim, P.R.J. 2005a. The global intelligence and security environmental sustainability model: Counteracting organized crime and international terrorism. *The Second CAMIS Security Management Conference: Managing Complexity and Developing Partnership Initiatives*, Birkbeck College, University of London, 23 September 2010.

Trim, P.R.J. 2005b. The GISES model for counteracting organized crime and international terrorism. *International Journal of Intelligence and CounterIntelligence*, 18 (3), 451–72.

Trim, P.R.J. and Lee, Y-I. 2006. Vertically integrated organisational marketing systems: A partnership approach for retailing organisations. *Journal of Business and Industrial Marketing*, 21 (3), 151–63.

Trim, P.R.J. 2009. Collaborative security: Pointers for government representatives and corporate security personnel, in *Strategizing Resilience and Reducing Vulnerability*, edited by P.R.J. Trim and J. Caravelli. New York, NY: Nova Science Publishers, Inc., 91–101.

Trim, P.R.J. and Caravelli, J. 2007. Counteracting and preventing terrorist actions: A generic model to facilitate inter-government cooperation, in *Terrorism Issues: Threat assessment, Consequences and Prevention*, edited by A.W. Merkidze. New York, NY: Nova Science Publishers, Inc., 135–52.

Trim, P.R.J., Jones, N. and Brear, K. 2009. Building organisational resilience through a designed-in security management approach. *Journal of Business Continuity & Emergency Planning*, 3 (4), 345–55.

Trim, P.R.J. and Upton, D. 2010a. Protecting Critical Information Infrastructure: Keeping up with the threats, *European Corporate Security Association (ECSA) Academy*, Dolce La Hulpe, Brussels, Belgium, 23 March 2010.

Trim, P.R.J. and Upton, D. 2010b. Emergency response simulation system research: Research into cyber security – current and future issues and Alternative Worlds, *Crisis Management Exercise Design and Development Workshop – Advanced*, Cranfield Resilience Centre, Cranfield University, Shrivenham, 3 June 2010.

Upton, D. 2007. Official crisis simulations in the UK and elsewhere, in *The International Simulation & Gaming Research Yearbook: Volume 15: Effective Learning from Games & Simulations*, edited by P.R.J. Trim and Y-I Lee. Edinburgh: SAGSET, 70–88.

Upton, D. 2009. Some suggestions for making emergency response exercises more consistent and more successful, in *Strategizing Resilience and Reducing Vulnerability*, edited by P.R.J. Trim and J. Caravelli. New York, NY: Nova Science Publishers, Inc., 197–212.

Watson, N. 2005. Europol: Form, function and implications, *The Second CAMIS security Management Conference: Managing Complexity and Developing Partnership Initiatives*. Birkbeck College, University of London, 23 September 2005.

Winston, R. Lord. 2011. Scientists & Citizens. St George's House Annual lecture 2010. *St George's House Annual Review, 2009–2010*. Windsor: St George's House, Windsor Castle, 4–11.

Websites

See http://www.us-cert.gov/aboutus.html [accessed: 23 November 2010].

See http://www.enisa.europa.eu/act/ar/deliverables [accessed: 23 November 2010].

See http://www.enisa.europa.eu/media/press-releases/cyber-europe-2010-a-successful-2019cyber-stress-test2019-for-europe [accessed: 23 November 2010].

See http://www.warp.gov.uk/warps-explained.html [accessed: 23 November 2010].

See http://www.skyboxsecurity.com/sites/default/files/CaseStudy_Actionable RiskMetricsFISMAAutomation_August2010.pdf [accessed: 24 November 2010].

4

Protecting Critical Information Infrastructure: Issues and Considerations

4.0 Introduction

The UK government body charged with providing protective security advice, the Centre for the Protection of National Infrastructure (CPNI), has an immense task. Many Critical Information Infrastructure (CII) providers rely on other suppliers, some of them outside the UK, and on relationships with government agencies inside and outside the UK. This may lead to problems from global competition and competition between public and private sectors, and to problems in sharing data. Business and regulators can have uneasy relationships. Some Critical Information Infrastructure Protection (CIIP) models involve state-run defence (e.g., Germany), while others (e.g., the US) have more private sector participation.

This chapter starts with a general overview (Section 4.1) and continues with issues and considerations relating to CIIP (Section 4.2). This is followed by wider implications and the public and private sectors (Section 4.3); strategic framework (Section 4.4); and placing matters in context (Section 4.5). Next there is a focus on cyber attacks (Section 4.6) and this is followed up with working towards a possible solution (Section 4.7). A conclusion (Section 4.8) is then provided.

4.1 General Overview

The UK strategic framework for CIIP was published in draft by the Cabinet Office in late 2009, and nine CII key sectors were identified. Regulatory systems are different, and there are issues around how they can be monitored. But there is a great need to understand the interdependencies between the sectors, and not to plan and prepare in isolation. Deliberate cyber attacks, by countries, hackers or insiders, represent a major and continuing threat. If successful, they can erode our confidence in our systems but do not have to destroy the systems altogether.

With respect to establishing which models and responses are appropriate for dealing with such attacks it is important to bear in mind that co-operation between organizations, both public and private, and across national boundaries, is to be encouraged as the severity and pace of attacks is increasing. A report by the ICE draws attention to areas where systemic changes are needed. CPNI, the Civil Contingencies Secretariat, and others have made a start. Our project looked particularly at exercises as a means of training, plan validation and communication between organizations. At the moment CIIP does not appear to have the strong 'exercise culture' found in other areas (e.g., COMAH). The research outcome from the project provided a firm basis upon which 'Alternative Worlds' was developed and resulted in exercises being easier to write and use, and had the added benefits of making exercises more realistic and systematic, by introducing elements of simulation into the design process.

The main focus of the research was to relate aspects of emergency management, disaster prevention and recovery management, and it is for this reason that a number of broader management issues were addressed and are included in the book.

We sought to identify the main stakeholders, the key responders and various ways forward with respect to what needs to be done, by whom and at which point in time, in order that CII is made more resilient through emergency management, disaster prevention and recovery management policy recommendations. Policy recommendations relating to training and staff development programmes that underpin the skill enhancement process of those involved can be strengthened through evidence based research. This should have the additional advantage of providing new insights into CIIP and/or helping those managing the research project to set priorities which both underpin the concept of Critical Information Infrastructure Continuity Planning and make it more effective, in a strategic context.

Organizational learning and context specific management processes and systems were considered and a number of quotations appear in the work. It is hoped that they add depth to our understanding and interpretation of what is a complex and under researched area of study.

4.2   Issues and Considerations Relating to Critical Information Infrastructure Protection (CIIP)

According to Hyslop (2007: 32):

> *Critical Infrastructure can be damaged, destroyed or disrupted by deliberate acts of terrorism, natural disasters, negligence, accidents or computer hacking, criminal activity, and malicious behaviour.*

It is clear that both the type and nature of a threat, the level of threat and the degree of vulnerability a nation is exposed to, cannot be easily quantified as the nature of the threat changes from time to time. Those intent on causing damage and/or disruption are not necessarily playing to any known rules of rational behaviour and are capable of using psychological and manipulative behaviour. The nature of a perceived threat changes from time to time and through time, but currently there are five key areas of Critical Information Infrastructure that need attention: connectivity, hosting, security, hardware and software (Hyslop 2007: 62). Owing to the processes of globalization, connectivity and interdependency, both the new and emerging business models and practices that are being developed are likely to provide those concerned with systems security with a demanding workload for the foreseeable future.

The Centre for the Protection of National Infrastructure (CPNI) is 'the Government authority for protective security advice to the national infrastructure relating to national security threats' (Cabinet Office 2009: 24). CPNI has an immense task with respect to continually informing and updating the various publics, about the existing and changing nature of threats that exist/ are likely to exist in the future. How these threats can be overcome or indeed eradicated is difficult to determine when one considers that those involved in them (directly or indirectly) represent a diverse grouping of individuals and organizations. Overseas government agencies, organized criminal syndicates, terrorist networks, activists and disgruntled individuals/employees are stretching the resources of the intelligence and security services, and indeed law enforcement and private security companies.

4.3   Wider Implications and the Public and Private Sectors

New business models such as outsourcing and offshoring bring new risks. It is hoped that senior managers have undertaken a risk assessment and are aware of what might go wrong and if it does, how the contingency plans once activated will reinforce and support the Business Continuity Planning process. However, it may not be realistic to expect that an adequate risk assessment has been made or will be made every time by a company, a government facility and indeed the community that are relying on an overseas CII provider or key services provided by an overseas company. Although it may be possible to identify who the owner of the CII provision is, it is possible that the provider, for commercial or national reasons, may have a private agenda. This may involve gathering intelligence, enhancing competitiveness or challenging rival enterprises. It may also have a strategic objective, namely the acquisition of resources/assets. Also, the fact that there is competition between private and public sector organizations (resources, personnel, technical support, prestige for example), makes it less certain how some governments will, in the future, be prepared to make resources available, if, that is, geo-political factors determine a change in the status quo or a realignment of CIIP policy. The energy issue is likely to refocus alliances and result in priorities changing as a consequence of increased global competition and more intense competition between private sector organizations.

Achieving sustainability through competitive advantage, however defined, is an important consideration for top management and outsourcing and offshoring provide for this. As interdependency increases between companies and nations, one should not think that the political risk is less than it was before because interdependency will in itself bring about tensions and conflict between nations. The asymmetric threats recognized by the security service (e.g. terrorism, weapons of mass destruction, organized crime and espionage), need to be placed in the context of Critical Infrastructure and Critical Information Infrastructure (Hyslop 2007: 179–80) provision. In other words, events that are beyond the control of a single government will be viewed differently by other countries because their priorities change/will change as they become less able to control events. Willis et al. (2009: 340) have stated that:

> The vast majority of infrastructure facilities are owned and operated by private interests. As a result, infrastructure risk management requires cooperation between the public and private sector. One area in which this is particularly true is in the sharing of information about risks

to infrastructure, especially international man-made risks such as terrorism.

If terrorists carry out an attack on a nation's infrastructure, co-operation and information sharing across the sectors will be necessary, by public and private sector personnel. However, there are a number of problems. Willis et al. (2009: 342) state:

> *Collecting information from the private sector requires coordinating, organizing, and analyzing thousands of disparate information feeds. Local, state, and federal law enforcement face challenges when sharing classified intelligence from the top down and incident reports from the field up. Finally, the public sector faces another set of challenges when considering how to share insight from classified and unclassified intelligence with the private sector.*

Willis et al. (2009: 343–4) have outlined why senior managers in the private sector need to make strategic, operational and tactical decisions, and note that they think in terms of *processes* as opposed to *facilities*. This is because of the nature of the business undertaken and also the type of business model deployed, which is very much about company–environment fit. What is clear is that security officers have a clearly defined role to play and work with law enforcement officers when required; and corporate staff rely on security professionals for advice with respect to 'how security impacts enterprise risk management' (Willis et al. 2009: 344). It seems that corporate staff are not interested in receiving classified information from government agencies but are interested in receiving information which 'is able to provide an assessment of the credibility of the information' (Willis et al. 2009: 346). In other words, the type of data/information supplied by a government department that is likely to be of value to an organization is that which is current and accurate, and which can be interpreted from the organization's immediate needs. For example, a government department may possess information relating to how a technology in a given market is evolving, but what personnel in a company require is likely to be receiving the data/information in a structured form that will allow in-house experts to interpret the data/information from a business impact perspective for example.

It can be noted that, while security professionals through their networks are able to receive and exchange information of a sensitive nature, within an organization only people of a certain level or responsibility may have access to secret and/or confidential data and information. The reasons why corporate staff are reluctant to share information is due to four factors (Willis et al. 2009: 346):

1.   Proprietary information may be leaked to competitors;

2.   If company vulnerabilities become public then customers or investors may defect elsewhere;

3.   The company may be liable in some way; and

4.   The risk associated with voluntary disclosures which result in regulatory procedures.

One has to be careful however. Data and information required by government is different to that required by corporations competing head-to-head. Bearing this in mind, a distinction needs to be made between government intelligence and corporate commercial data. A key consideration is the role played by intelligence and security officers, and law enforcement officers, and the laws which govern their way of operating. So information has a different value attached to it and is used in different ways. Security clearance is an issue and needs to be tackled if that is information is to move between interested parties (Willis et al. 2009: 354). One way forward is to think in terms of producing information of a useful nature and linking it with analysis and the information flow needs to be in both directions (public and private sectors) (Willis et al. 2009: 362) as represented by the Information Exchanges managed by CPNI in the UK.

   Bearing the above points in mind, it is relevant to place the subject of CII Protection within the governance theory body of knowledge as it involves co-operation and co-ordination (Pommerening 2004: 7) and public accountability. What is interesting about Pommerening's (2004: 22) work is that there appears to be similarities and differences between the US and Germany as regards CII Protection. Pommerening (2004: 22) states: 'The U.S. clearly has a more elaborate private sector organizational structure responding to cyber threats, while CIIP in Germany is largely attached to state-run civil defense mechanisms'. Possibly the most useful consideration to emerge from this interpretation is that a stakeholder model needs to be inclusive and have a designed-in security dimension. The work of Trim et al. (2009) is useful with respect to this way of thinking as it links security work with Business Continuity Planning.

4.4 Strategic Framework

The October 2009 draft publication entitled 'Strategic Framework and Policy Statement on Improving Resilience of Critical Infrastructure to Disruption from Natural Hazards', proposes 'a cross-sector programme to improve the resilience of critical infrastructure and essential services to severe disruption by natural hazards' (Cabinet Office 2009: 3).

The purpose of the Strategic Framework and Policy Statement 'is to establish a shared, consistent, proportionate and risk-based approach to delivering reductions in vulnerability over a number of years, as envisaged by Sir Michael Pitt in his reports on the floods of Summer 2007' (Cabinet Office 2009: 6). The main emphasis appears to be to develop a co-ordinated approach to improve the resilience of Critical Infrastructure by identifying and assessing risks, and to develop a range of options in order to 'avoid, transfer, accept, reduce or share those risks' (Cabinet Office 2009: 6).

Critical National Infrastructure (CNI) has been defined as:

> *Those infrastructure assets (physical or electronic) that are vital to the continued delivery and integrity of the essential services upon which the UK relies, the loss or compromise of which would lead to severe economic or social consequences or loss of life (Cabinet Office 2009: 9).*

The European Union defines Critical Infrastructure in the following way:

> *A critical infrastructure (CI) consists of those physical and information technology facilities, networks, services and assets which, if disrupted or destroyed, have a serious impact on the health, safety, security or economic well-being of citizens or the effective functioning of governments (Cabinet Office 2009: 9).*

According to the President's Commission on Critical Infrastructure Protection, 1997 (Pommerening 2004: 1), Critical Infrastructures have been defined as 'infrastructures which are so vital that their incapacitation or destruction would have a debilitating impact on defense or economic security'. Hence the relationship between public and private sector organizations is undergoing structural change (Pommerening 2004: 1) and this is likely to intensify as governments realize that CII is firmly embedded in 'the global communications infrastructure' (Pommerening 2004: 5). There are reasons for this structural change, namely: the process of privatization and investment by the private sector in previously state owned activities; the need for capital to find more lucrative returns than previously as some industries reach maturity; the insatiable demands associated with consumerism and how it acts as a stimulus and fosters technologically driven products and services; the process of globalization and the standardization of technologies and products across industrial sectors; and the concentration of expertise in various business models that are well able to exploit current and future technological and infrastructural opportunities.

There are nine national infrastructure sectors (Cabinet Office 2009: 9; Cabinet Office 2010: 24): energy, food, water, transportation, communications, emergency services, health care, financial services and government (see Tables 4.1 and 4.2). As regards regulation, it is noted that the health sector, the emergency services sector and part of the transport sector, are regulated differently to the water and energy sectors, and because of this, a different approach is needed in order to ensure that these sectors deliver the aims listed in the programme outlined by the Cabinet Office (2009: 23; Cabinet Office 2010: 9).

Bearing this in mind, the appointment of a CIO (Chief Information Officer) within an organization should ensure that information security is an integral part of the strategic management process and this being the case, CIIP will be more complete (Hyslop 2007: 106). Corporations can ensure that they participate fully in CII protection by appointing a Chief Information Officer/ Chief Security Officer at board-room level, and can be considered an aspect of Corporate Governance (Cukier 2005: 43). The issues of compliance and governance are integrated and not thought of as separate entities, and will no doubt focus attention on relevant industry standards and the work of the regulatory bodies. For example:

> The ability to respond effectively to security events will depend on the ability to monitor and detect security related events and the quality of the response plans in place. This in turn is dependent upon well secured and monitored systems, effective and clear governance and the skills and awareness of personnel (CPNI 2007: 5).

Referring back to work undertaken by the Cabinet Office (2009 and 2010), it can be noted that key areas of focus include areas of investment needed to improve the level of resilience so that the Critical Infrastructure is improved and meets

Table 4.1   The nine national infrastructure sectors with associated sub sectors

National Infrastructure Sector	Sub Sector	Whitehall Sector Sponsor Dept	Lead in Scotland	Lead in Wales	Lead in Northern Ireland
Communications	- Telecommunications	BIS	BIS	BIS	NIO
	- Postal Services	BIS	BIS	BIS	
	- Broadcast	DCMS	DCMS	DCMS	
Emergency Services	- Ambulance	DH	SE	WAG	NIO
	- Fire & Rescue	DCLG	SE	WAG	NIO
	- Marine	DfT	DfT	DfT	NIO
	- Police	HO	SE	HO & WAG	NIO
Energy	- Electricity	DECC	DECC	DECC	NIO
	- Gas				
	- Fuel				
Finance	- Payment, Clearing & Settlement Systems	HMT	HMT	HMT	NIO
	- Markets & Exchanges	HMT	HMT	HMT	NIO
	- Public Finances	HMT	HMT	HMT	NIO
Food	- Production	DEFRA & FSA	SE	WAG & FSA	NIO
	- Processing				
	- Import				
	- Distribution				
	- Retail				
Government	- Central government [1]	CO			NIO
	- Devolved Administrations/Functions;		SE	WAG	NIO
	- Regional & Local government;	CLG	SE	WAG	NIO
	- Parliament	Palace of Westminster Authorities [2]	Scottish Parliamentary		

Table 4.1   Continued

National Infrastructure Sector	Sub Sector	Whitehall Sector Sponsor Dept	Lead in Scotland	Lead in Wales	Lead in Northern Ireland
Health	-Health & Social Care	DH	SE	WAG	NIO
Transport	-Aviation	DfT	DfT	DfT	DfT/NIO
	-Maritime	DfT	DfT	DfT	DfT/NIO
	-Land	DfT	SE (road)	WAG-(road)	NIO (road+rail)
Water	-Portable Water Supply	DEFRA	SE	WAG	NIO
	-Waste Water Services				
	-Dams				

Key:

BIS: Department for Business, Innovation and Skills, CLG: Department for Communities and Local Government, CO: Cabinet Office, DCMS: Department for Culture, Media and Sport, DECC: Department of Energy and Climate Change, Defra: Department for Environment, Food and Rural Affairs, DfT: Department for Transport, DH: Department of Health, FSA: Food Standards Agency, HO: Home Office, HMT: Her Majesty's Treasury, NIO: Northern Ireland Office, SE: Scottish Executive, WAG: Welsh Assembly Government.

[1] 'And reserved functions thereof such as Defence and National Security'.
[2] 'Although not a Whitehall government department, these authorites lead on the security of Parliament'.

Source: Cabinet Office 2010: 24. Reproduced with permission from the Cabinet Office, London (Crown Copyright).

Table 4.2   Criticality scale for national infrastructure

Criticality Scale	Description
CAT 5	This is infrastructure the loss of which would have a catastrophic impact on the UK. These assets will be of unique national importance whose loss would have national long-term effects and may impact across a number of sectors. Relatively few are expected to meet the Cat 5 criteria.
CAT 4	Infrastructure of the highest importance to the sectors should fall within this category. The impact of loss of these assets on essential services would be severe and may impact provision of essential services across the UK or to millions of citizens.
CAT 3	Infrastructure of substantial importance to the sectors and the delivery of essential services, the loss of which could affect a large geographic region or many hundreds of thousands of people.
CAT 2	Infrastructure whose loss would have a significant impact on the delivery of essential services leading to loss, or disruption, of service to tens of thousands of people or affecting whole counties or equivalents.
CAT 1	Infrastructure whose loss could cause moderate disruption to service delivery, most likely on a localised basis and affecting thousands of citizens.
CAT 0	Infrastructure the impact of the loss of which would be minor (on national scale)

Source: Cabinet Office 2010: 25. Reproduced with permission from the Cabinet Office, London (Crown Copyright).

the higher standards proposed for dealing with UK climate projections; and at the same time facilitate the development of Critical Infrastructure sector resilience plans – which allows the work to be placed within a resilience-building framework that takes into account 'the differences between sectors and regulatory regimes' (Cabinet Office 2009: 3). Hence it is essential to ensure that the 'dependencies and inter-dependencies within and between sectors are highlighted and targeted' (Cabinet Office 2009: 3) and as a consequence, the vulnerability associated with CIIP will be reduced.

A key point noted by Verton (2003: 20) is that infrastructure system providers do not appear to understand the interdependencies among the systems in being and the problem is made worse by the fact that staff at central government, local government and local utilities, sometimes write their response plans in isolation. Brenner (2009: 49–50) has indicated that in February 2006 the US Department of Homeland Security's Cyber Storm exercise revealed that organizations that were defending themselves against the attack found it difficult to co-ordinate their attack response between the public and private sectors and the different public sector agencies. This is a key concern that needs to be addressed and guidance provided.

4.5 Placing Matters in Context

The following example outlines some of the problems associated with CIIP. It is drawn from Cukier (2005: 9), and relates to the September 11 terrorist attack on the US, highlighting both the vulnerability and resilience associated with information infrastructure, and the interdependence of the existing networks:

> After the second plane crashed into the South Tower at 9:02am, telephone calls increased up to ten times the normal traffic volume – so much congestion that only a handful could get through. Major news Web sites – CNN, the BBC, The New York Times and others – were so clogged with traffic they became temporarily unreachable. By 9:39am many radio stations in the city went dark (most broadcasters had transmitters in the towers). When the first tower collapsed at 10:05am, and then the second at 10:28am, they destroyed the vast amount of telecom infrastructure in the vicinity, complicating communications even more … network technicians struggling to repair systems coordinated their activities using mobile text messages since their cell phones couldn't handle calls. And as many noted afterwards, the Internet worked when the phone system didn't. Indeed, at 9:54pm the Federal Emergency Management Agency alerted all stations to prepare in case primary communications methods failed – and did this, ironically, by email.

Cukier (2005: 9) noted that:

> the actual event did not do too much damage to the information infrastructure – yet subsequent problems with other networks began to cause havoc. For instance, a fire at a building on the periphery of the World Trade Centre knocked out a power station upon which telecoms equipment elsewhere depended. A falling beam from an unstable building in the vicinity crashed into an operator's central switching office, damaging the machines. By late evening, systems that had survived went down simply because they overheated. And telecom services were disrupted when backup generators ran out of fuel because trucks carrying new provisions were blocked from entering lower Manhattan.

Another important point is speed. What really causes concern, is that CII protection is 'decentralized, interconnected, interdependent and controlled by multiple actors (mainly private) and incorporating diverse types of technologies' (Cukier 2005: 14). Key issues are the cost of CII protection; who bears the costs and what do they get in return; and how can the stakeholders shoulder responsibility for cost. Again, the national versus international dimension of the problem surfaces.

During the recovery phase of the September 11 attack on the World Trade Center, Cukier (2005: 27) stated that:

> after the attack, around 200,000 telecom circuits were down, 3.6 million data lines went out, 10 cell sites were destroyed and service was off for 40,000 businesses and 20,000 residential customers. The result? Emergency responders (police, firefighters and ambulances) received priority service and their communications never experienced interruption; the roughly 1.5 million data lines and 2 million telecom circuits that comprise the stock exchanges were operational within days. Business service was restored quickly, and eventually, residential service fully back within three months, not a matter of years.

4.6   Cyber Attacks

Brenner (2009: 1–12) has outlined clearly the cyber attacks that were unleashed on Estonia over a period of two weeks in April/May 2007, and suggests that botnets have also been used to attack the Netherlands and the US for example. It has also been reported that possibly government involvement may have been used to engage in cyber warfare and cripple another country's infrastructure with the intent of paralyzing its government and economy (Brenner 2009: 65). Although the Estonian authorities indicated which government they believe orchestrated the attacks, Brenner (2009: 7) concludes that Estonia may never be able to prove who organized the attack and why it was unleashed upon the country in the way that is was, and this suggests that cyberspace is presenting policy makers with 'a behavioural dimension rather than a spatial dimension' (Brenner 2009: 9). Such events suggest that 'Real-world warfare is overt and destructive; cyberwarfare will be subtle and erosive' (Brenner 2009: 10), and this is reason enough for organizations in the public and private sectors to co-operate by sharing information and devising joint actions plans.

According to Brenner (2009: 42 and 48):

*cyberterrorism seeks to erode our confidence in the constituent
infrastructures that are essential for our security and survival in
modern, urban societies ... terrorists launch a psychological attack when
they use computer technology as a weapon of mass distraction; the goal
is to undermine civilians' confidence in one or more of the systems they
rely on for essential goods and services. The cyberterrorists accomplish
this by making citizens **believe** a system has been compromised and is
no longer functioning effectively. The terrorists do not actually impair
the functioning of the system. Their goal is to inflict psychological, not
systemic, damage ... on one or more target system.*

According to Verton (2003: 23) those involved in preventing or rectifying attacks
on CII need to have an understanding and an appreciation of knowledge relating
to critical assets, vulnerabilities and operational dynamics. Furthermore, Pollitt
(Verton 2003: 27), states that:

*Cyber-terrorism is the premeditated, politically motivated attack
against information, computer systems, computer programs, and data
which results in violence against non-combatant targets by subnational
groups or clandestine agents.*

So the issues involved are wide ranging and so are the possible solutions. Attacks
carried out by insiders also need to be considered as part of the equation, and
will no doubt continue to feature in news stories. Verton (2003: 27) has made
clear the problem by stating that:

*in November, 2001, a 49-year-old Australian man was sentenced to two
years in prison for using the Internet and stolen control software to
release up to one million litres of raw sewage into public parks and
creeks throughout Queensland, Australia's Sunshine Coast. The man,
who had been a consultant on the water project, conducted the attack
after he was refused a job with the company that installed a computerized
sewage system for Maroochy Shire Council. The creek water turned
black, and an untold number of precious marine animals died. More
telling is the fact that the facility failed to notice the attacker's 44
previous break-in attempts.*

Another example from Verton (2003: 28) can be cited:

*In 1997, a teenage hacker disabled a key telephone company computer,
cutting connectivity to an airport in Worcester, Massachusetts.*

Although the teen had little or no knowledge of what he had done, the airport control tower lost critical services for six hours, forcing incoming airplanes to rely on radio communications and other airports to provide landing instructions. That same year, a technician at a Virginia Internet service provider inadvertently injected errors into the ISP's routing tables, causing critical Internet routers to crash.

4.7   Towards a Possible Solution

The work of Suter (2007: 1) suggests that CIIP models need to be placed in a national context and also, the complexity involved will differ from one country setting to another hence the models 'are not always necessarily applicable to other countries'. Suter (2007: 1) also states that 'many existing solutions are fairly resource-intensive and therefore not suitable for the majority of countries in the world'. Pommerening (2004: 1) also makes the point that the difference between the US model and the German model is due to the difference in state systems.

Examples such as these do raise a number of questions and it is not surprising that senior managers are left wondering what constitutes best practice? And also, how can all the stakeholders be involved in the process? A possible solution is at hand. Suter (2007: 1–4) proposes a generic, Four-Pillar Model of CIIP:

a)   Prevention and early warning;

b)   Detection;

c)   Reaction; and

d)   Crisis management.

(A) PREVENTION AND EARLY WARNING

The main aim is to reduce, by whatever means, the number of information security breaches and incidents that an organization is confronted with. Managers can reduce the organization's level of vulnerability by adopting recommendations and guidelines relating to best practice; by preparing responses in relation to warnings of specific threats, and this is done in a timely manner; and by implementing training and carrying out exercises. This will require managers to assess the risk involved and make trade-offs.

(B) DETECTION

New or emerging threats (technical and/or criminal organizations) need to be identified in advance and a national and international network can assist with this from the stance of sharing intelligence/information through co-operation, which is underpinned by trust-based relationships.

(C) REACTION

It is important to identify and correct the causes of disruption; however, CIIP needs to be viewed from the perspective of complementing what organizations do and not providing complete solutions. A key point to note about incident response is that 'many attacks are carried out by international actors, companies often do not know how to secure appropriate law enforcement responses abroad. The CIIP unit should support targeted companies by referring them to the responsible authorities' (Suter 2007: 3). Knowledge can be shared through lessons learned and this would be advantageous with respect to improving crisis planning. Indeed, organizations can compare emergency plans and take, with the support of government, action to avoid making mistakes.

(D) CRISIS MANAGEMENT

CIIP plans must involve key decision-makers in organizations and government. This means that all the organizations responsible for conducting emergency exercises as well as relevant government bodies are required to know what their responsibilities are, and to ensure that they are able to deal with the risks as they manifest in a time of crisis.

*****

As regards preparing responses in relation to warnings of specific threats (prevention and early warning – point A above), it is worth mentioning that there are too many of these and as a consequence, an organization's resources and skills may be deployed in a continual and inefficient manner. However, it is better to have countermeasures in place than to be caught off guard and/or unable to respond to an incident in real time. Damage limitation is sometimes the best approach and at times the only approach. With respect to new or emerging threats being identified in advance (detection – point B), this it has to be said is rarely possible. In the case of reacting to a disruption (point C), governments can help by co-ordinating international reactions and acting on behalf of national companies. It is also worth pointing out that during a crisis (point D) a crisis management plan must be comprehensive and robust enough to work as expected.

Suter (2007: 5–6) has outlined a CIIP co-operation model which is composed of three main partners:

a) A governmental agency (the head of the CIIP unit provides strategic leadership and supervision);

b) An analysis center (known as the Situation Center – it has strong links with the intelligence community); and

c) A technical centre of expertise (composed of staff members of CERT (Computer Emergency Response Team)).

As regards strategic leadership and supervision, Suter (2007: 5) suggests that the CIIP unit be situated within a well-established agency and that the head of the unit is well grounded in ICT (especially information assurance) or in Critical Infrastructure protection. The head of the unit needs to have the confidence of the private sector and be able and willing to work with private sector organizations. It is argued that various components of the intelligence service should be partners of the CIIP unit and the universities, which have research strengths and technical expertise, should co-operate and work in partnership with the CIIP unit (Suter 2007: 6). It is also suggested that the head of the Situation Centre should possess legal and political knowledge and his/her staff should be engaged in a number of duties including mentoring CII operators and helping them raise public awareness (Suter 2007: 8). Managers must be able communicators and the CERT team must be fully aware of what information assurance involves and be capable of dealing with early warnings. It has been suggested that the most important members of the CIIP unit are the owners and operators of Critical Information Infrastructures (Suter 2007: 9).

In order to ensure that information sharing takes place, it is suggested that formal agreements are entered into and it is advised that non-disclosure agreements are put in place, and a number of classification levels of information are defined (Suter 2007: 14). Suter (2007: 15) states:

These classification levels enable companies to limit the spread of information. Of course, it should always be the information source who decides on the classification, and the information may only be re-classified with their agreement. This rule is fundamental and should be observed at all times.

Suter (2007: 15) observes, and observes correctly, the fact that legislative measures may be needed to enable information sharing to take place. The OECD (2007) report entitled *Development of Policies for Protection of Critical Information Infrastructures*, is highly informative as regards information sharing at an international level. For example, reference is made to seven countries and the fact that in the countries surveyed, 'the national risk management framework is a combination of organizations, processes and government standards leading to actions to manage risk and improve the protection of critical information infrastructure' (OECD 2007: 14). Bearing this in mind it is not surprising to learn that a number of factors militated against sharing information across borders, for example various sensitivities resulted owing to legal issues in relation to data protection; law enforcement and in particular cyber crime activities; and culture itself, which linked the concept of a security culture with the pressures exerted by technology (OECD 2007: 26).

CPNI (2007: 6) have advocated the creation of a Process Control Security Response Team (PCSRT) which is:

a core element of an organisation's response capability and provides the foundation for effective monitoring, analysis and managing the response to alerts and incidents. The PCSRT must be involved at every step in the process of monitoring a situation, analysing any changes to the cyber threat and initiating appropriate responses.

It is suggested that members of the PCSRT could be drawn from: process control, SCADA, automation teams; IT security; IT infrastructure; business management; operations; internal regulators; the legal department; corporate media contact; and the corporate security team (CPNI 2007: 7). The advice provided by CPNI (2011: 15–16) should be well received by managers in organizations that are intent on establishing their own PCSRT and also, such a team can operate at a high level within an organization and across functional areas.

The CIIP unit will need to find a number of competent partners to allow it to deal effectively with a number of eventualities (Suter 2007: 18). What is clear, is that attacks manifest in different forms and are of different intensity. It is for these reasons that a partnership approach may often help to detect an attack before it has had a chance to cause a great deal of damage/disruption.

By isolating the problem, those dealing with the attack are giving themselves time to limit the damage/disruption caused and to put in place countermeasures to prevent further attacks. Indeed, it may be that various overseas governments need to be informed about the situation and/or the co-operation of overseas law enforcement agencies is needed. A number of questions can be posed: Are the necessary co-operative law enforcement procedures in place? Are additional co-operative law enforcement procedures necessary? Organizing and administering effective incident response programmes is key if that is a threat is to be neutralized and those responsible for the attack are to be prevented from doing so again. It needs to be remembered that there are fairly good co-operative agreements in place between most countries, however, two exceptions can be noted:

1.   Developing countries may be prepared to collaborate, but are not sufficiently resourced to do so effectively; and

2.   'Rogue' countries may not be prepared to co-operate effectively, even though they may claim to do so.

It is useful at this point to reflect and to take into account the in-depth assessment of defending the UK's critical infrastructure produced by The Institution of Civil Engineers (ICE) in 2009. The Institution of Civil Engineers report makes compelling reading. The report cites four main recommendations:

1.   *We recommend that the government creates a single point of authority for infrastructure resilience to coordinate the work of the agencies responsible for dealing with individual sectors and threats and recognize interdependency. This would provide the fundamental overview that is lacking, consider how to fill in gaps and address the areas of infrastructure defence which are currently ignored.*

2.   *With climate change identified as the biggest threat currently facing the UK's infrastructure, government must ensure that the newly created Natural Hazards Team is effective. Government should invest the Natural Hazards team with the power to provide*

strong leadership to asset owners and ensure legislation is properly enforced.

3. *Government must give clearer guidance to sector regulators such as Ofgem and Ofwat. At present these regulators' remit is largely the short-term prices by end users. In order to deliver the improvements to resilience identified as necessary by government and the overview function for infrastructure resilience, regulators must have the capacity to address asset resilience as well as broader and longer term consumer interests. Regulators require the ability to ensure asset owners build in reserve capacity to critical infrastructure and that they are fully prepared for any emergency scenario.*

4. *The circuitous UK planning system has long delayed the delivery of many crucial pieces of infrastructure. Government must ensure that the Planning Act 2008 and the Infrastructure Planning Commission (IPC) effectively reform the planning system for major infrastructure. Without reform the UK is in danger of not having the infrastructure it needs to operate (ICE 2009: 4).*

As regards the vulnerability of UK networks, three examples can be cited which bring home the separate but related issues as regards resilient networks and infrastructures. They are drawn from the ICE (2009: 7) report entitled *The State of the Nation: Defending Critical Infrastructure*, which in turn draws upon a number of sources.

Example 1: System failure

In May 2008 people living in London, Cheshire, Merseyside and East Anglia, were affected by blackouts when the Sizewell B nuclear reactor and the Longannet coal-fired power station, unexpectedly stopped working and as well as people being and businesses being affected, essential services such as the fire brigade were sent out on what turned out to be false alarms.

Example 2: Climate change

In 2007, the Mythe water treatment works in Gloucestershire flooded and for 17 days, the water supply of 350,000 people was cut off. As a result of the floods, 5 water treatment works and 322 sewage treatment works became non-operational and 40,000 people in Gloucestershire were, for a 24-hour period, left without power.

Example 3: Terrorism

In the morning rush hour of 7 July 2005, widespread disruption was caused when bombs were exploded on three London underground trains and a bus; and as a result 52 people were killed as well as four suicide bombers, and a further 700 people were injured.

It has been reported that:

The current approach to increasing infrastructure resilience is disjointed and piecemeal. There is a lack of overview, a lack of coordination, there are issues with funding, regulation and planning and an overall failure to recognize interdependency (ICE 2009: 8).

Referring to the valuable work undertaken by CPNI, the Natural Hazards Team (Cabinet Office Civil Contingencies Secretariat), the Met Office and the Environment Agency, it has been noted that the work carried out:

focuses on individual aspects of resilience and operates within different departments. In addition, on a day-to-day basis, agencies, local authorities, regulators, asset owners, and the emergency services all work separately in their individual regions and sectors, with little scope for sharing information or joint forward-planning (ICE 2009: 8).

Sharing information seems appropriate given the issues at stake and CPNI (2007: 16) recognize that managers may be inclined to keep process control security incidents confidential; however:

Sharing such information can allow further investigation by other agencies, the avoidance of similar incidents in other organisations and develop a better understanding of the risks facing control systems (CPNI 2007: 16).

It is also clear that more has to be done in the area of training, and in particular that exercises can be used to develop and update emergency response skills (Lee et al. 2009). In other critical national areas, such as health and safety, an 'exercise culture' already exists. (For example, the Control of Major Accident Hazards, or COMAH. legislation, obliges the operators of large, potentially dangerous sites such as oil refineries, and the authorities and agencies in their area, to hold regular joint exercises.) Such a culture brings several benefits:

1.   Response plans are more co-ordinated and therefore more effective;

2.   Plans are regularly tested and validated;

3.   The responders involved get to know, understand and trust each other, making for better information flow and quicker joint action, as well as a more realistic understanding of each others' strengths and weaknesses;

4.   A mechanism is in place for disseminating new ideas and information; and

5.   All concerned are regularly reminded, in a dramatic way, of the threats that exist.

The use of exercises is advocated in the CIIP context: for example the CPNI's (2007: 6) 'Good Practice Guide' on Process Control and SCADA Security says:

> *Obtaining management support, determining responsibilities, establishing communication channels, drafting policies, and procedures, identifying pre-defined actions, providing suitable training and exercising the whole process prior to incidents enables a quick, effective and appropriate response which can minimise the business impacts and their cost, possibly avoiding such incidents taking place in the future.*

However, we are not sure how often such exercises are actually held. The most widely known CIIP exercises are the US-led but multi-national Cyber Storm series. According to the official Australian report on Cyber Storm II (Attorney-General's Department, Australian Government 2008), this was the first national level CIIP exercise held in Australia. Planning took 18 months; 12 scenarios were involved, and the exercise lasted 4 days.

The EU Ministerial Conference on CIIP (EU Presidency 2009: 5) concluded that 'A joint EU exercise on CIIP should be organised and staged by 2010, in line with the Commission's action plan'. As in Australia, this is also a first step:

This joint endeavour would be the first tangible step towards a strong coordination and cooperation among Member States as well as help identify areas requiring immediate actions (EU Presidency 2009: 5).

It is good to report that the joint EU exercise on CIIP has been held.

Clearly exercises on this scale are new, and cannot be held often. We do not know how often similar but more limited exercises are held, for example by individual companies or groups of companies and agencies. Part of the purpose of this research project is to make such simulations easier and more accessible on a smaller scale.

Relatively little academic work appears to have been undertaken on the simulation of CIIP activities, using the word 'simulation' in the more mathematical sense of modelling relationships within complex systems. Rinaldi (2004) has a good understanding of the problems involved, including difficulties obtaining data, the fact that individual infrastructures are complex and give rise to interdependency problems (physical, cyber, geographic and logical); and problems with reconciling the different assumptions made in the models used reflecting the very complex and inter-dependent set of relationships involved. Rinaldi (2004: 5) points out:

simulations could be used to develop realistic training scenarios that accurately mirror the effects of disruptions [...and...] could enhance the fidelity, content, and value of exercises and training.

In the US, the National Infrastructure Simulation and Analysis Center (NISAC 2009) 'conducts modeling, simulation, and analysis of the nation's critical infrastructure' and its analysts 'assess critical infrastructure risk, vulnerability, interdependences, and event consequences'. It is encouraging to note that NISAC benefits from the sharing of information between the public and private sectors, and the expertise of its staff is used in the areas of risk mitigation and policy planning.

In the EU, the DIESIS project (Design of an Interoperable European federated Simulation network for critical InfraStructures) has been looking at the feasibility of establishing a European Infrastructures Simulation and Analysis Centre (EISAC). Masucci et al. (2009: 1) discuss linking areas of education and training, with CII policy formulation and implementation, and argue for developing a Knowledge Base System (KBS) to 'discover new inter-dependencies among critical infrastructure models'.

Neither of these appears to address the other purpose of our own research project, namely to make tentative steps towards bringing more rigour into exercise design, by using more explicit simulation techniques as advocated by Rinaldi (2004).

4.8　Conclusion

The UK has a highly skilled and committed group of people, drawn from both the public and private sectors that are determined to face up to the issues and problems relating to the protection of Critical Information Infrastructure. The journey that we have embarked upon is uncertain and may be more problematic than we first thought; however, our determination and combined strength will ensure that adequate disaster and emergency plans are put in place, and that the subject of Critical Information Infrastructure Continuity Planning is given a higher standing than is the case at present. It is envisaged that as a result of our combined efforts, the security body of knowledge and indeed the body of knowledge relating to emergency planning and disaster management will be enriched. In turn, this should result in universities in the UK being more involved in this type of work and more committed to providing relevant programmes of study for those that wish to update their knowledge and skill base or those that wish to embark on a career in one of the related areas of study outlined above.

References

Attorney-General's Department, Australian Government 2008. *Cyber Storm II: National Cyber Security Exercise: Final Report*. Available at: http://www. ag.gov.au/www/agd/agd.nsf/Page/Publications_CyberStormII-September 2008 [accessed: 31 December 2009].

Brenner, S.W. 2009. *Cyberthreats: The Emerging Fault Lines of the Nation State*. Oxford: Oxford University Press.

Cabinet Office. 2009. *Strategic Framework and Policy Statement on Improving Resilience of Critical Infrastructure to Disruption from Natural Hazards*. (Draft-October Natural Hazards Team, Civil Contingencies Secretariat). London: Cabinet Office.

Cabinet Office. 2010. *Strategic Framework and Policy Statement on Improving the Resilience of Critical Infrastructure to Disruption from Natural Hazards*. (March Natural Hazards Team, Civil Contingencies Secretariat). London: Cabinet Office.

CPNI. 2007. *Good Practice Guide: Process Control and SCADA Security: Guide 3. Establish Response Capabilities.* London: Centre for the Protection of National Infrastructure (CPNI). Available at: http://www.cpni.gov.uk/Docs/Guide_3_ Establish_Response_Capabilities.pdf [accessed: 31 December 2009].

CPNI. 2011. *Cyber Security Assessments of Industrial Control Systems: A Good Practice Guide.* London: Centre for the Protection of National Infrastructure (CPNI). Available at: http://www.cpni.gov.uk/documents/ publications/2011/2011apr28-infosec-cyber_security_assessments_of_ics_ gpg.pdf [accessed: 31 May 2011].

Cukier, K. 2005. *Critical Information Infrastructure Protection: Ensuring (and Insuring?): A Report by The Rueschlikon Conferences.* (September). Rueschlikon: Switzerland.

EU Presidency. 2009. Conference conclusions. *European Union Ministerial Conference on Critical Information Infrastructure Protection.* Tallinn, Estonia, 27 to 28 April, 2009. Available at: http://www.tallinnciip.eu/doc/EU_Presidency_ Conclusions_Tallinn_CIIP_Conference.pdf [accessed: 31 December 2009].

Hyslop, M. 2007. *Critical Information Infrastructures: Resilience and Protection.* New York, NY: Springer.

ICE. 2009. *The State of the Nation: Defending Critical Infrastructure.* London: Institution of Civil Engineers.

Lee, Y-I., Trim, P.R.J., Upton, J. and D. Upton. 2009. Large emergency-response exercises: Qualitative characteristics – A survey. *Simulation & Gaming: An International Journal of Theory, Practice and Research,* 40 (6), 726–51.

Masucci, V., Servillo, P., Dipoppa, G. and Tofani, A. 2009. Critical Infrastructures ontology based modeling and simulation. Chapter of a book. Available at: http://www.diesis-project.eu/include/Publications/paper.pdf [accessed: 31 December 2009].

National Infrastructure Simulation and Analysis Center (NISAC). 2009. Available at: http://www.dhs.gov/xabout/structure/gc_1257535800821. shtm#2 [accessed: 31 December 2009].

OECD. 2007. *Development of Policies for Protection of Critical Information Infrastructures.* Ministerial Background Report DSTI/ ICCP/REG(2007) 20/FINAL: Paris: OECD. Available at: http://www.oecd.org/dataoecd/ 25/10/40761118.pdf [accessed: 31 May 2011].

Pommerening, C. 2004. A comparison of critical information infrastructure protection in the United States and Germany: An institutional perspective. Paper presented at the *Annual Meeting of the American Political Science Association,* Chicago, 2 September 2004, 1–30. Available at: http://www. allacademic.com/meta/p60905_index.html [accessed: 10 November 2009].

Rinaldi, S.M. 2004. Modeling and simulating Critical Infrastructures and their interdependencies. *Proceedings of the 37th Hawaii International Conference on*

System Sciences – 2004, 1–8. Available at: http://www.computer.org/plugins/ dl/pdf/proceedings/hicss/2004/2056/02/205620054a.pdf?template=1&login State=1&userData=anonymous-IP%253A%253A87.80.20.41 [accessed: 31 December 2009].

Suter, M. 2007. *A Generic National Framework for Critical Information Infrastructure Protection (CIIP)*. (August). Zurich, Switzerland: Center for Security Studies.

Trim, P.R.J., Jones, N. and Brear, K. 2009. Building organisational resilience through a designed-in security management approach. *Journal of Business Continuity & Emergency Planning*, 3 (4), 345–55.

Verton, D. 2003. *Black Ice: The Invisible Threat of Cyber-Terrorism*. Emeryville, CA: McGraw-Ill/Osborne.

Willis, H.H., Lester, G. and Treverton, G.F. 2009. Information sharing for infrastructure risk management: Barriers and solutions. *Intelligence and National Security*, 24 (3), 339–65.

5

Critical Information Infrastructure: Methods of Conceptualizing Interdependencies that No One Person Fully Understands

5.0 Introduction

Information infrastructure systems are highly complex and very interdependent. Traditional ways of describing these interdependencies are not always helpful, partly because the complete spectrum of knowledge required to fully comprehend the complexities involved is rarely available in one organization or institution. Effects-based methods, and models, also have serious limitations.

We describe each transaction as a 'stack' of several layers, all of which are relevant to the transaction. In most cases each 'single' transaction is actually many transactions. The continual evolution and changeable nature of the internet in particular means that it is impossible to say in advance which way a transaction will be made, at almost any point in the stack. Rather than trying to build a better model that encapsulates all the possible outcomes and solutions needed, we believe that we have to live with systems as 'black boxes', many of which most users do not understand, even though they can be understandable. We argue for a 'bottom-up' approach to conceptualizing and training system owners and users, which looks at the needs of users and tries to meet them by methods such as simulation. By achieving this, we will be able to develop more appropriate solutions to common problems, and advance user understanding of what is a very complex subject.

A number of interrelated issues and topics are covered in this chapter. First, attention is given to what is known as traditional analysis (Section 5.1) and this is followed by effects-based analysis and modelling (Section 5.2). Next, attention is given to the layered approach (Section 5.3) and this is followed with a piece relating to protean systems (Section 5.4). The 'black box' model is referred to (Section 5.5) and this is followed by the 'bottom-up' approach (Section 5.6), and then a conclusion (Section 5.7).

5.1   Traditional Analysis

It is clear that there is a high level of interdependency among the systems that make up Critical Information Infrastructure (CII). However, the situation is extremely complex and often confusing, even for experts. For CII to be properly understood and made resilient, it is important that 'generalist' users, not just technicians and systems experts, should have sufficient understanding of these interdependencies to be able to manage business systems securely, to specify them correctly, and to make sensible decisions in an emergency, if their organizations are to be resilient. One of the issues confronting managers in organizations today, is that if they have a generalist background, they may not know exactly how the information systems in the organization work or may possess partial knowledge only. At the very least they need to know:

1.   How to tell when their systems may be going wrong;

2.   Where to turn for help in their own organization;

3.   Which other organizations may be affected, or able to help;

4.   What issues to consider when specifying and managing information systems; and

5.   How to provide information to external organizations, e.g., industry associations or government departments and agencies.

Infrastructure interdependencies have been categorized in several ways, to make it easier to identify, understand and analyse them. As a starting point, Rigole and Deconinck (2006: 2) refer to a four-fold division.

5.1.1   PHYSICAL

Physical interdependencies are those in which one infrastructure depends on outputs of the other. For example, a telephone system cannot work if the 'last mile' of copper wire to a house has been brought down. Much of our infrastructure is buried underground, and despite the best efforts of owners and the authorities, is regularly damaged by contractors. Electrical and water supplies are interrupted by bad weather, bringing down pylons or cracking pipes. The BT tunnel fire in Manchester in 2004, which brought chaos to the surrounding area, is another good example.

5.1.2   CYBER

Cyber interdependencies are those in which the state of an infrastructure depends on the information transmitted through an ICT infrastructure. For example, transmission of oil along a pipeline depends on a digital signal telling the system that the tank at the other end still has room for more.

5.1.3   GEOGRAPHIC

Geographical interdependency is similar to, but looser than, physical interdependency. For example, the breakdown of public transport systems in a large city would affect businesses in the city, even though there is no direct connection between the two. Work on Geographic Information System based models is useful as it 'is intended to help government agencies plan for the knock-on effects that propagate between major infrastructures' (Johnson and Williams 2008: 1).

5.1.4   LOGICAL

Logical interdependencies represent a more complex concept. Rigole and Deconinck (2006) refer to policy, legal or regulatory interdependency. It is more difficult to think of examples. Airport legislation in the UK, for example, requires a specified amount of fire service coverage: so if this is unavailable, the airport is obliged to stop operations, even though there is no direct impact on its ability to handle traffic. Although the rules are less clear-cut, many industrial activities such as oil refining would probably have to stop if some safety systems were unavailable, and these in turn depend on information systems, e.g., to report when storage tanks are overfilling. (The reader will recall the Buncefield disaster was caused by the over-filling of a storage tank.)

5.2 Effects-based Analysis and Modelling

There have been other approaches. Instead of the four categories Rigole and Deconinck (2006) suggest, Zimmerman (2004) uses a database of utility failures to derive a matrix showing which types of infrastructure most frequently damage other infrastructures when they fail, and which are most frequently damaged. In other words, he does not attempt to describe reasons (e.g., physical or cyber dependency) but simply looks at the facts: What failures lead to other failures? He produces a matrix showing the interdependency ratios of his data sample.

In Zimmerman's (2004) study, water mains were the most likely to cause damage, gas mains the most likely to be damaged. 'Electric lines' and 'cyber/fibre optic/telephone' lines were among the least likely to cause damage or to suffer it from others. However, his sample was small and his work experimental: he does not claim to have identified ratios which would apply everywhere.

More detailed studies have been made of electrical power systems. For example, Ren and Dobson (2008) use nine years of historical data for regional electric power transmission. Although in one sense these data only relate to a single type of network, Ren and Dobson still find that 'Cascading failures that arise in practice can be very complicated chains of events and often include unanticipated interactions or rare events'. Ren and Dobson (2008) use the figures to develop and demonstrate a new method of predicting statistically how far outages are likely to spread, given certain initial data.

Another study by Mackin et al. (2007) argues that a thorough fault tree analysis of every possible network node would rapidly become unmanageably large. Therefore, in order to realistically predict most interactions, they use critical node analysis to identify key points or nodes in a network, and then to weight them. Their study uses network analysis techniques, identifying the nodes with the most connections, since 'more connected nodes have a bigger impact on the overall system than less connected nodes' (Mackin et al. 2007). The authors then suggest that resilience efforts should be focused on the most connected nodes. Their study is based on an oil pipeline system, which adapts well to this sort of analysis. Information infrastructure does not, for reasons we will set out shortly. (Though they do claim that a similar approach has been applied to the internet.)

Studies like these attempt to classify infrastructure components by the effects of their possible failure, either looking backward from observed effects without making a priori causal judgements, or using network techniques to simplify and Pareto-optimize the huge range of causal judgements that could be made.

Other categorization systems quoted by Rigole and Deconinck (2006) include:

a)   The infrastructure environment (technical, business, political and legal for example);

b)   The couplings among the infrastructures and their effects on their response behaviour (loose or tight, inflexible or adaptive);

c)   The infrastructure characteristics (organizational, operational, temporal, spatial);

d)   The state of operation (normal, stressed, emergency, repair), the degree to which the infrastructures are coupled; and

e)   The type of failure affecting the infrastructures (common cause, cascading, escalating).

Bearing these points in mind, it is clear that there is no simple way to express dependencies. This is recognized by Rigole and Deconinck (2006) who state:

> *This inherent complexity clearly shows one important design tradeoff in modeling; the more low-level details in our model, the more accurate it should be, but the more complex (in design and computational complexity) it becomes. Modeling at a higher abstraction level may lead to simpler models, but aggregate high level behavior may be very hard to model and as such be inaccurate.*

A great deal of effort has been put into modelling, and making simulations of network interdependencies, using common simulation technologies, for example:

1.   Discrete steps.

2.   Agent based modelling.

3.   Neural or evolutionary methods.

There are lists of relevant CIP 'Simulations, Tools and Software' available on the internet (for example, see http://www.chds.us/?media/resources&collection=53&type=SIMULATION), and there are numerous simulation projects under way. However, all so far seem to be daunted once they step outside the narrow limits of a single subsection of their system, by the extreme complexity of the subject they are modelling. As Rigole and Deconinck (2006) state (quoted above), there is a trade-off between complexity and accuracy. Simple models are easy to make, but not always very accurate. Complex models are much more difficult to make, and it is many times more difficult to make sure that they have included all the right equations.

Second, it is difficult to be certain that any schema, model or simulation is in fact 'accurate'. There is even a whole literature on what 'accuracy' means in this context (Drennan 2005), and how to 'verify' models (Moss 2008). It is generally agreed to be dangerous to use simulations to make predictions in 'soft science' environments. In order to have confidence in a simulation, you need to understand the underlying system as well as the model in some detail.

Models have a clear, but finite, range of uses: Rigole and Deconinck (2006) provide ten examples, including:

- Discover weak spots in existing infrastructures to optimize future investments.

- Optimize deployment of limited resources (medicines, rescue workers, tents …) for emergency response teams in case of catastrophic events, such as hurricanes, earthquakes or large scale terrorist attacks.

- Study the social impact of large scale power blackouts.

Rigole and Deconinck's (2006) list also includes 'let autonomous intelligent control agents distributed over the power grid infrastructure use a state estimator to learn the best action taken in both steady state (operational optimization) and critical scenarios (minimize consequences of failures)' adding cautiously that 'some believe such systems will be far more effective than when a human supervisor needs to react to failure events'.

A third issue is up-to-date information. Even if any given model were to be shown to be completely representative today, it is highly likely, given the revolutionary times we are living through, that it will be inaccurate tomorrow. Only someone who controlled the whole system, and could enforce reporting of every change, could hope to be aware of every development in the system.

Nevertheless the ideal of a 'model of everything' continues to flourish – for example the EU DIESIS project lists many single-sector simulation packages and some which take a national viewpoint (DIESIS 2008), and Masucci et al. (2010), a DIESIS collaborator, has proposed:

> a Knowledge Base System (KBS), a virtual layer that acts internally to a federated simulation environment. The KBS enables the dynamic binding among different Critical Infrastructures models.

Whether such models are really possible, and how we would know if one was accurate and reliable if it could be built, are beyond the scope of this chapter. (The US defence community has made considerable efforts to 'join up' their plethora of simulation models, but it is not yet clear whether these attempts have been successful.)

Psychologically, simulations and models offer a possible means of side-stepping the complexity by referring it back to the machines that made it, but this neat solution may be dangerously short-sighted. It is akin to admitting that no one can understand these systems, or at least that no one can understand them in real time, and therefore relinquishing control of one system to another system.

This is not necessarily a bad thing. For example, the Eurofighter is inherently unstable – no human pilot could keep it in the air. Its control systems react more quickly than a human, and make stable flight under the overall direction of a human pilot possible. Clearly this works, since these aircraft fly well. But Eurofighters are (if we may say so) relatively simple systems compared to CII. They do not, for example, fly in the air at one moment and underground the next. They are not jets for one millisecond and Zeppelins for another.

The title of this chapter is, we think, literally true in the sense that we are dealing with a collection of systems that no one (i.e., no one person) fully understands. They can be broken down into intellectual fiefdoms, such as networks, TCP/IP, operating systems, radio propagation, cryptography and security for example. Some people may understand one or two of these very well, but, although some exceptional people may have a good understanding of all of them, such polymaths are few and far between. Even the experts are specialists. This is partly because the sheer complexity of each area makes it difficult to master more than one or two. There are also organizational dynamics: working in one area does not give opportunities to find out about another. Employers want to focus training and experience on the systems which they themselves sell, and even the largest customers cannot afford enough experts to duplicate the support they expect the manufacturers to provide. As practitioners, we have seen several cases where control and support of a complex system is farmed out to various contractors and suppliers, each responsible for one small part of it, while the overall 'manager' has only limited technical knowledge. Sometimes systems are proprietary or classified, and it is not possible for outsiders to understand them fully.

Problems occur at interfaces. It is easy to imagine situations in which two separate systems are both working well, but have become incompatible. (As a mundane example, regular updates to Microsoft operating systems sometimes cause unexpected problems for software working on those systems.)

5.3   A Layered Approach

For our purposes, it may be more useful to look at networks from a layer perspective. Any network transaction involves interaction on several layers, often referred to as a 'stack'. These may include:

1.   The actual 'physical' means of making a connection (e.g., copper wire, fibre, which may be low bandwidth local nets, or high bandwidth 'backbones', or wireless, which in turn may involve local transmitters, or satellites).

2.   The protocols used to connect (e.g., packet data or circuit switching). A circuit switching network is one that establishes a circuit or channel between nodes and terminals before the users may communicate, as if the nodes were physically connected with an electrical circuit. Packet switching is the process of segmenting a message/data to be transmitted into several smaller packets. Each packet is labeled with its destination and the number of the packet, precluding the need for a dedicated path to help the packet find its way to its destination. Each is dispatched and many may go via different routes. At the destination, the original message is reassembled in the correct order, based on the packet number.

3.   The software and hardware which facilitate the interface (e.g., telephone exchanges, Internet routers and DNS servers, space satellites).

4.   The content – this may be analogue or digital data. Modern digital data can include almost anything: speech, data, images and music for example. It may be changed back and forth during the process of transmission, e.g., when digital signals are turned into analogue by a modem for transmission along telephone lines, or when analogue signals are 'sampled' in order to save bandwidth by trimming out frequencies which human ears cannot experience. With the growth of 'smart' electric power networks and wireless chargers, energy itself may also become a form of 'content'. Fabrication technology also holds out the possibility of recreating real objects over a network.

The user interface and the use to which the network is put. (For example, public telephone networks or PSTN, an NHS internal data network, GIS systems, private company LANs, etc.) A 'typical' connection appears in Figure 5.1.

Figure 5.1   Typical connection

One result of the current communications revolution is that it is becoming increasingly difficult to make assumptions about which layers will be used. For example, telephone systems (PSTN) once transmitted analogue voice signals over copper wires via electro-mechanical telephone exchange switches. Now telephone conversations may use VOIP (i.e., internet) systems, and a single conversation be carried via satellite internationally, by microwave radio transmissions nationally, and by cable or wire for the 'last mile'. Internet data can be carried over power lines (broadband over power line, or BPL), telephone systems, or wireless systems. Power lines which once had their own private network of process control wiring may now rely on wireless internet signals, and so on.

The closer Critical Information Infrastructure comes to the dynamics of the internet, the more complex it becomes. The internet is deliberately decentralized, and offers multiple paths between any two points. The system is allowed to find its own paths between nodes. This is a major advantage, since the network becomes fault tolerant: if one node goes down, the network automatically routes around it. However it also means that at any given moment, users may have no way of knowing how their data is being moved, and even less control over whether (for example):

1. The actual connection is wireless, fibre or wire (in practice it may use all three), let alone which actual circuits are being used;

2. What facilitating software/hardware is being used (e.g., which DNS server – hence Twitter's recent problem with the 'Iranian Cyber Army' which hijacked its DNS servers and rerouted its traffic.) 'Cloud' services add to this confusion;

3. Which connection protocol is being used (e.g., VOIP); and

4. Whether their content is sent as data packets or as switched circuits.

At first sight, the system only seems predictable at the user interface level – i.e., the box you have on your desk. However, the user interface itself can be further broken down into layers. For example:

1. Operating system (e.g., Windows, *nix, etc.). One organization may use several different systems (e.g., one or more older versions of Windows for process control software, and Unix for internet access). A conversation on a corporate LAN may use several of these.

2. Data services may be internal or external databases. Internal databases traditionally sat on a private server in the corporate computer rooms. Internally owned databases may be hosted on different types of RDBMS with different vulnerabilities (e.g., SQL Slammer only affected one type of RDBMS). It is not uncommon for legacy systems to mix different data sources, with interfaces between them, so that the data required for a single transaction may be spread over several machines and systems. Many 'single' database transactions also interact with external public databases such as Google Earth, or payment systems such as PayPal. Some databases are 'outsourced' across the internet, e.g., to services like Amazon's SimpleDB. Often systems use a mix of data sources, e.g., emergency response services using external GIS data with their

own databases. Database software of the future may move towards the REST model, in which data is held even more flexibly.

3.   Internal networks and LANs. Typically, organizations have their own LANs based on commercial software such as Lotus Notes or Windows. Different sections of the same LAN may use different servers and even different software. The LAN may also introduce another 'layer of layers' if it allows VPN access to outside workers using the internet. Human LAN users are perhaps the worst offenders, inadvertently opening their systems up to intruders such as Ghostnet.

4.   User-facing applications may vary from user to user within an organization (e.g., some may use Internet Explorer browsers, some Firefox). Many modern applications need Internet access to look up other protocols, e.g., XML DTDs, or rely on 'web services' such as externally hosted group calendars. A 'single' web page may be making a large number of requests to the internet (e.g., for supporting files, or for data via AJAX). The growth of coding styles such as .css and non-intrusive Javascript means that viewing a single web page is likely to involve downloading other pages. Increasingly, even the 'user application' (see Figure 5.2) may itself be an externally hosted web service, e.g. Google Tools.

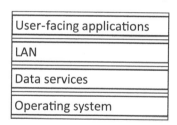

Figure 5.2   User application

We have therefore expanded our 'road map' to show these layers (Figure 5.3).

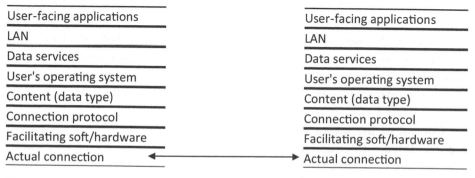

Figure 5.3   Extended connection

This connection is repeated many times over as each 'packet' of data is sent, and the details may change with each one. Each layer may have some degree of 'choice' over the operation of the layer beneath it, and it may choose differently each time it sends a 'packet' or a message. In addition, as each packet moves from one place to another, it repeats the lower layers of this diagram with each 'hop'. Here, for example, is the route taken by a single request from the author's PC (in London) to the BBC News website (also in London):

```
212.58.226.75 is from United Kingdom(UK) in region Western Europe

TraceRoute to 212.58.226.75 [newslb306.telhc.bbc.co.uk]
```

Hop	(ms)	(ms)	(ms)	IP Address	Host name
1	18	21	7	72.249.0.65	
2	15	8	6	64.129.174.181	64-129-174-181.static.Twtelecom.net
3	14	19	46	4.69.145.243	ae-92-90.ebr2.dallas1.level3.net
4	8	22	29	66.198.2.37	if-5-0-0-31.core2.dtx-dallas.as6453.net
5	50	53	53	4.69.134.114	ae-64-64.csw1.newyork1.level3.net
6	42	41	41	4.69.134.65	ae-61-61.ebr1.newyork1.level3.net
7	124	115	239	216.6.42.74	if-5-0-0-908.core1.fr1-frankfurt.as6453.net
8	114	115	138	80.231.64.90	if-11-1659.har1.fr1-frankfurt.as6453.net
9	127	122	146	80.81.192.59	rt-decix.fft.bbc.co.uk
10	143	121	129	212.58.238.133	
11	143	141	128	212.58.239.58	
12	160	136	122	212.58.226.75	newslb306.telhc.bbc.co.uk

This single request has travelled from the UK via the US and Germany and back to the UK in 12 'hops', each requiring a restatement of the lower layers of the stack. An identical request made a few minutes later did not route through Germany. Note that the time taken is measured in milliseconds, and to a human user all these decisions seem to have been taken, and these distances traversed, instantaneously. Streaming a short video from the BBC News website would involve thousands of packets coming back via a similar route – or a mixture of routes. Compare this to the flow of oil down a pipeline (Table 5.1).

Control of the layers is also more complex. This is obvious, e.g., from reports (Privacy International 2003) of attempts by nations to censor or limit internet access in the UAE, where it seems that, despite the government enforcing internet access only through a single company, the need to have and

Table 5.1   A comparison of oil and data flows

Oil	Data
Route is as direct as possible, because of high cost of laying line.	Route is indirect; in effect there is no additional costs to taking a longer distance.
Usually sent as one single transaction.	Split into parts and sent as very many separate transactions which probably follow different routes.
Takes hours or days.	Takes fractions of a second.
Usually there is only one possible route, which is set up in advance.	Can take many routes: which is determined at the time.
Systems are simple to understand (valves, pipes) even though they may be complex to optimize.	Needs complex systems to split the data into packets, route it, and to reassemble the data at the receiving end.

configure several proxy servers lead to inconsistencies in what could and could not be seen. Partly because of privatization and competition policies in many developed countries, communications monopolies are difficult to enforce. In authoritarian states, attempts to control such things as internet access are at best flawed, and tend to 'throw the baby out with the bathwater' – that is, they limit useful access as well.

5.4   Protean Systems

Proteus was a Greek God, described by Homer in the Odyssey. He could foretell the future and help mankind in many ways, but would change his shape and disguise himself, in order to avoid having to do so. This ability to change shape is typical of modern CII, making Proteus an ideal metaphor for modern systems. They bring great benefits, but they resist being pinned down and made to offer clear explanations of themselves.

In many ways this 'Protean', fault-tolerant nature overcomes some of the traditional problems with information infrastructure. Taking out one part of the network may not interfere with it. At worst, it may slow the network down as information crowds other routes. At best it may not even be noticed. It also offers other benefits: the network can be more flexible if bottlenecks can be automatically routed around. It can grow in modular fashion, without central planning. However, it brings its own set of problems. The first, as noted above, is complexity. Individual chunks of networks may be modelled quite satisfactorily, but an overall model of how, for example, an internet page request goes from London to London, may be more complex. At best a model can assign probabilities to the many possible options, or it can identify the more vulnerable options. But it can never tell you exactly what 'will happen', because this is usually not predictable.

Protean systems bring their own practical problems which face users every day. For example:

1. When disruption is at a low level and the network handles it adequately, but then starts to slow down as the disruption increases and fails suddenly when it reaches a critical mass;

2. When part of the network is operating incorrectly, but fools the rest of the network (e.g., the recent attack on Twitter). This ability is often used in disaster recovery simulations, for example, to allow a backup system to take over from the 'main' system which is deliberately switched off to provide a test. The rest of the system is switched over to talk to the backup system, and if this is working satisfactorily, everything continues as before; and

3. When the disruption is so intense that even the fault-tolerance fails, or a single point of failure is found (e.g., SQL Slammer).

Networks are not, of course, infinitely Protean. In some cases 'self-healing' may only delay diagnosis of a problem until it has become large enough to swamp the limited alternatives. In other cases the network options may be very limited (which is why you can consider controlling internet access in the UAE, but not in the UK). However, because of the Protean nature of networks, we believe that it is becoming increasingly difficult to predict if, how and when a network will fail, or even to understand how it has failed. Hence the number of simulations and models being developed, and the increasing areas they cover as they attempt to cater for all possible strategies a network may devise to self-heal. Once again comparison with an 'old-fashioned' network, such as oil supply pipelines, makes the point clearer. Any given point (say a storage terminal) is usually only served by one pipeline. Pipelines are expensive to build and maintain, and there are social issues involved in laying them down across the country. The 'switches' which control the flow of oil along and between them are very much physical pieces of machinery (pumps, valves, etc.) with definite purchase and maintenance costs, rather than pieces of software which have a different economic model. At any given point there is usually only one switch, whereas internet signals may go through many different makes of router. Oil industry alternatives (e.g., moving oil products in road tank trucks if a pipeline shuts) are prohibitively expensive or impractical. Although the control network which supervises the physical network may be 'Protean' to some degree, the physical network is very limited and a single accident to a major line may cause serious problems.

5.5   The 'Black Box' Model

For every CII user, the system (s)he uses is at some stage a 'black box'. Even if it is possible, we doubt whether anyone actually does have the degree of knowledge, or the time, to be aware of every step a complex system is taking, and to understand it in depth. The 'black box' model assumes broadly that:

1.   At one or more stages in the process, my data or transaction disappears into/emerges from a 'black box'. (For most people, and for many generalist managers, the 'black box' starts just behind their PC keyboard.)

2.   Usually, I do not expect to understand fully what is inside the box, although I may have some expectations about its behaviour.

3.   I assume that someone somewhere knows what is happening inside the box, even though this may be a false assumption. For example, the box may be setting its own rules, e.g., a router finding a route for a data packet. Or, the person who once understood how the box worked may have moved to another job. (From our experience with industrial systems, this is more common than you would expect.) Thirdly, it is possible that the box may be managed by somebody who only has an imperfect understanding of how it should work. (Firewalls are sometimes cited as a good example. It is difficult for generalist managers even to understand what qualifications are needed to set a firewall, let alone to know if it has been properly set.)

It may even be possible that the behaviour inside the black box is in some sense unknowable, like Schroedinger's cat. Historically we can know what a system did at some time in the past, if we take the time and trouble to analyse its logs in detail. But in 'real time', even the expert is often acting largely on intuition. The system may be 'deterministic', but the actual result may depend on many factors (e.g. the order in which requests came in, or the external environment), which mean that its decisions cannot in practice be predicted. Even for 'experts' who have a good understanding of one of the black boxes, it is often the case that the others are closed to them. As we argue above, these are separate fiefdoms. What is required is not an expert knowledge of the inside of another 'black box', but an awareness of what to do when it is part of a system which has become problematic. The key is to manage sensibly, and to ensure that the protection in place is both adequate in the short term and sustainable in the long term.

5.6   A 'Bottom-up' Approach

We have argued that there are three problems with any overall descriptive framework or 'top down' simulation technology. Firstly, it is bound to be complex. This may be acceptable for machine use, e.g., to build control loops into a complex system, which can then monitor itself and 'self-heal'. However, humans are not able to handle much complexity, and need something simpler. Our own preference is for a 'bottom-up' approach as a means of:

1.   Enabling humans to grasp something of the complexities of the CIIP environment, outside their own areas of specialization;

2.   Training them to better understand their own corner of that environment, and how it may typically interact with the areas next door (e.g., different functions within the organization);

3.   Helping them to recognize the early signs that something is going wrong;

4.   Helping them to work with others inside and outside their organization to remedy the situation; and

5.   Helping them to specify and manage systems intelligently.

The trainers' objective is to produce teams and people who can:

1.   Notice and identify signs that there may be a problem;

2.   Alert managers and clients;

3.   Take emergency action, e.g., to shut down systems or isolate them if necessary. (This is often a very difficult judgement, almost always made with inadequate information. Over-reaction can make the problem much worse than it need be.)

4.   Take early steps to manage the way the problem will affect their organization and those who rely on it, including bringing 'workarounds' into play or rationing services, and discussions with suppliers; and

5.   Establish and use links with other affected bodies, to make sure that responses to the problem are co-ordinated.

Actually identifying and repairing the underlying cause of the problem may take time, and is usually left to system engineers or other experts. (With SQL Slammer, for example, this involved developing an anti-virus patch, installing it, cleaning affected systems, and bringing them back online. The attack was over in minutes – the resolution took days.) In other words, it is not always necessary to understand an attack completely in order to make a successful emergency response.

A second problem with the 'top down' approach is that the response teams and the individuals who compose them often need to work with others, rather than in silos. In the SQL Slammer case, most actions were taken by individual organizations – for instance, network managers who shut down whole networks as the worm multiplied. Some of them contacted others informally, but there was no time to co-ordinate decisions. SQL Slammer was perhaps unusual in the speed and extent of its spread, but we believe that most organizations still react in a 'self-centred' manner – that is, they read signals from their own systems, and act individually to optimize their own system performance. In some cases this is because they are not sure who to contact in other organizations, or how to contact them, and there may be no easy mechanism for making such contacts.

CERTs, WARPs and IEs are being set up to make such contacts easier. As well as providing a list of contact telephone numbers, they bring several advantages:

1.   A better understanding of 'neighbouring' systems – i.e., those you may affect, which may affect you, or which will suffer 'common cause' failures when you do.

2.   Personal contact with potential emergency responders from other organizations. This may sound like a luxury, but experience in other areas shows that it is invaluable when you are trying to put a response together quickly at 0200 on a Sunday morning.

3.   A source of advice.

At the moment the CERT/WARP/IE network is not complete and a major effort is required to complete it. One way forward is to recognize the fact that more attention needs to be given to the human factor with respect to identifying and solving CII related problems. Lee (2009) has reinforced the point that: 'No amount of technology can replace the human factor to want to investigate further, leverage instincts, and use reasoning abilities to further investigate an event'. Although government departments have done a great deal to make clear the fact that future threats are likely, the private sector needs to be more aware of how a company can fit within the co-ordinated response effort (Lee 2009: 131). It is essential therefore that managers in the private sector are aware of the range and intensity of potential attacks and design and put in place realistic response and recovery plans.

Our suggestion is therefore to use simulation systems 'from the bottom up'. That is, rather than try to simulate every possible interaction, to provide training simulations of plausible interactions, allowing those who have to work with these systems an opportunity to experience what can happen and what can be done to manage an incident. Typically, this involves exposing managers and users to 'exercises' or 'drills', in which they play through an incident step by step. The purpose is not to focus on the incident itself: for example, the simulation may show what has gone wrong, without explaining exactly why. Instead, the purpose is to take managers through the basic incident management steps, which we described above as:

1.   How to tell when their systems may be going wrong;

2.   Where to turn for help in their own organization;

3.   Which other organizations may be affected, or able to help,

4.   What issues to consider when specifying and managing information systems; and

5.   How to provide information to external organizations, e.g., industry associations or government departments and agencies.

What is therefore required is a system which is relatively simple to operate, so that it can be used by non-experts, but which can allow users to generate plausible training scenarios affecting their own CIIP systems. They can use these as they wish, as a means of:

1.   Raising awareness among non-specialists about issues;

2.   Helping them to plan to manage incidents; and

3.   Helping them to train incident response teams.

These are not new ideas: exercising and training are already used extensively in many industries and by many government agencies. The oil industry, for example, has a well-developed 'exercise culture' – managers expect to take part in 'emergency response' simulations and to use these to develop their ability to respond, at personal and corporate levels. However, exercises are not so widely used in the CIIP sector. Rigole and Deconinck's (2006) list of possible uses for simulations, which is quoted above, does not include training for incident management. We suspect this may partly be due to the complexity of writing such simulations. Such exercises should be simple to write and run, so that they can be held quickly and often without needing excessive preparation. They should come up with new challenges on a regular basis, to build confidence, to establish a habit of thinking around issues, and to lay down 'neural nets' within and between organizations. However, if the experts do not even agree on how to conceptualize interdependencies, how can you set about presenting a clear plausible picture of them? Also, given the range of expertise(s) required to understand all the component parts of a single transaction, few individuals can confidently provide a plausible model of the whole.

5.7   Conclusion

This chapter was prepared to accompany a workshop held at Birkbeck, University of London on 29 March 2010, as part of a programme funded by the Technology Strategy Board, to develop the 'Alternative Worlds' system. The idea behind the 'Alternative Worlds' system is in part to store separate expertise(s), and then to combine them easily and intelligently to write plausible exercise or simulation scripts. These simulations are not 'predictions': they are scenarios, but plausible scenarios used as learning tools. It is our view that such simulations will provide an excellent means of training users and managers to anticipate and cope with resilience issues and at the same time create an 'exercise culture' in and between their organizations.

References

DIESIS. 2008. *Report on Available Infrastructure Simulators*, DIESIS Project, 2008. Available at: http://www.diesis-project.eu/include/Documents/ Deliverable2.3.pdf [accessed: February 2010].

Drennan, M. 2005. The human science of simulation – a robust hermeneutics for artificial societies. *Journal of Artificial Societies and Social Simulation*, 8 (1) (January). Available at: http://jasss.soc.surrey.ac.uk/8/1/3.html.

Johnson, C.W. and Williams, R. 2008. Computation support for identifying safety and security related dependencies between national critical infrastructures. Available at: http://www.dcs.gla.ac.uk/~johnson/papers/ IET_2008/National_Critical_Infrastructure_Final.pdf [accessed: 5 February 2010].

Lee, E. 2009. *Homeland Security and Private Sector Business: Corporations' Role in Critical Infrastructure Protection*. Boca Raton, FL: CRC Press/Taylor & Francis Group.

Mackin, T.J., Darken, R. and Lewis, T.G. 2007. Managing risk in critical infrastructures using network modeling, in *Critical Infrastructure Protection: Elements of Risk: Critical Infrastructure Protection Program*, December. Arlington, VA: George Mason University School of Law.

Masucci, V., Adinol, F. and Servillo, P. 2010. *Critical Infrastructures Ontology Based Modelling and Simulation*. Available at: http://www.diesis-project.eu/ include/Publications/paper.pdf [accessed: February 2010].

Moss, S. 2008. Alternative approaches to the empirical validation of agent-based models. *Journal of Artificial Societies and Social Simulation*, 11 (15), (January). Available at: http://jasss.soc.surrey.ac.uk/11/1/5.html.

Privacy International. 2003. Silenced – the United Arab Emirates: Privacy International article, 2003. Available at: http://www.privacyinternational. org/article.shtml?cmd[347]=x-347-103788 [accessed: February 2010].

Ren, H. and Dobson, I. 2008. Using transmission line outage data to estimate cascading failure propagation in an electric power system. *IEEE Transactions on Circuits and Systems 2008*. Available at: http://eceserv0.ece.wisc.edu/ ~dobson/PAPERS/renCAS08preprint.pdf.

Rigole, T. and Deconinck, G. 2006. A survey on modeling and simulation of interdependent critical infrastructures, IEEE, *3rd IEEE Benelux Young Researchers Symposium in Electrical Power Engineering*, Ghent, Belgium, 27–28 April 2006.

Wired. 2010. Internal twitter credentials used in DNS hack, redirect, 18 December 2009. Available at: http://www.wired.com/threatlevel/2009/12/twitter-hacked-redirected [accessed: February, 2010].

Trim, P.R.J. and Caravelli, J. (eds). 2009. *Strategizing Resilience and Reducing Vulnerability*. New York, NY: Nova Science Publishers Inc.

Zimmerman, R. 2004. *Decision-Making and the Vulnerability of Interdependent Critical Infrastructure*, CREATE REPORT Under FEMA Grant EMW-2004-GR-0112, 10 October 2004. Los Angeles, CA: Center for Risk and Economic Analysis of Terrorism Events, University of Southern California.

Insights into Organizational Learning

6.0 Introduction

In this chapter, reference is made to data that was collected via a small group interview and through a questionnaire survey. Once collected, the data was analysed and interpreted. There were several objectives of the research. It was important to understand how organizational learning was perceived and how important it was with respect to influencing transformational organizational change. A number of factors were looked at including the role of exercises and whether exercises increased awareness and co-operation of staff across functions. Furthermore, evidence was collected regarding which type of organizational culture is suitable for dealing with cyber attacks. The chapter is composed of the following: organizational learning and a case study narrative (Section 6.1); a review and reflection of organizational learning (Section 6.2); a discussion (Section 6.3); and a conclusion (Section 6.4).

6.1 Organizational Learning and Case Study Narrative

A small group interview, composed of five people (two highly experienced exercise experts, a senior manager with extensive management and staff development experience, and two senior academics) and lasting 40 minutes, was held at Birkbeck College, University of London on 22 October 2010. The small group interview, which was in the form of a discussion, was tape recorded with the permission of those taking part. The interview was highly interactive and produced a large number of insights. The questions posed were drawn from the topics and the subjects that had emerged during the table-top exercises and the desk research. For example, during the workshops, it was noted that senior managers in the public sector viewed organizational learning differently from those in the private sector. As a result, a limited number of broad based questions were posed during the small group interview. They were: How do senior managers perceive organizational learning? How can senior managers integrate existing organizational held knowledge into an organizational learning model? How can organizational learning reinforce training and staff development within an organization? Is organizational learning partly to do with identifying future risks? Can organizational learning be used to devise a strategy to mitigate against the risks identified? How important is transparency with respect to holding people accountable for the decisions that they made? How relevant is organizational learning in the context of building organizational resilience? Can complex exercises be used to promote organizational learning? Can exercises help people to learn to communicate? What value does an exercise have?

The transcript of the interview was analysed on a line-by-line basis and a summary was produced. The summary, in the form of a narrative, is produced below.

6.1.1   ORGANIZATIONAL LEARNING CASE STUDY NARRATIVE

Managers in the public and private sectors work with different business models and because of this the concept of organizational learning is interpreted differently and there is no single view as to what organizational learning represents. It can be stated that knowledge sharing and the development of knowledge are handled differently, depending upon the industry in which the organization competes. Of key interest are: information sharing can be interpreted in various ways, the training of staff is important and the use of simulation exercises is common practice in complex industries. The best results using a simulation exercise are found in organizations that value organizational learning and have a dedicated workface.

Within organizations that embrace organizational learning, there are often discussions regarding the linkage of education and training, or how education can embrace training. A key consideration that senior managers want to answer is having had an exercise(s), how does the organization change? And if it does not change, why is it? If an organization makes a mistake(s) and does not change the way it operates, it cannot be defined as a learning organization.

There is a distinction between individual learning and organizational learning. Training is normally associated with individual learning and some organizations are better than others at integrating learning objectives into an organizational learning model. Some organizations have an organizational cultural value system which allows managers to ask: What have they done wrong during the exercise(s)? This is so that they can be told and they can put it right. In this type of organization, staff are very critical of what they have done and how they have done it. Staff in a learning organization write up lessons that reinforce both individual and organizational learning, and organizational learning is integrated within the organization's management systems and procedures. In other words, an individual's learning objectives are matched with the organization's learning objectives.

A learning organization culture requires that employees need to think of ways in which to improve and be more productive. If top management do not ensure that the organization's value system embraces change, then it is likely that staff lower down the hierarchy will not innovate and seek change. This is because junior managers consider it too risky to argue for new policies and procedures. Staff in some companies do not want to be told if they make mistakes, and instead want to be reassured that what they are doing is acceptable. In such organizations, people become defensive when they are told they could have performed better than they did. They will instead be inclined to support those in power and not challenge their authority. Those that do seek change may find that they are isolated and their career is put on hold. Sadly should this be the case, it is unlikely that the organization will adapt as quickly as it should and as a consequence the organization may lose its competitive advantage in the industry in which it competes. The only cure for companies with a silo mentality is often a forced restructuring, which is brought about by a failure to survive an external crisis. A restructuring normally that witnesses the introduction of a number of new management policies, and the appointment of new staff to senior management positions.

If there is no mechanism for controlling and recording knowledge within the organization then it is lost within the organization's memory. A learning organization ensures that people can and do document their views and knowledge, and that other organizational members have access to this knowledge bank (via an internal network).

The role of information and the value of the information within an organization needs to be linked with reputation management, which is being viewed as increasingly important with respect to limiting the effects of a disaster of any kind. Staff need to know the value of information and how it can be used in a beneficial sense. One measure of how a company handles a disaster is the resulting value of its shares. If managers do not handle a disaster well, the share value of the company is most likely to fall and this is a measure of confidence among stakeholders. During a crisis as opposed to a disaster, the CEO will need to be well advised as regards what is said to the media because there is a risk that a negative statement or a statement that is viewed as having negative connotations will affect the stock market value of the company. Alternatively, a high performing top ranked CEO may witness the share value of the company he/she joins increase as investors gain confidence in his/her ability to make the organization perform well/better than expected.

Organizational learning comes from the top. It requires top management to put in place the right organizational structure, embed the right attitude among employees and promote teamwork and information sharing. A problem can arise when people in an organization are competing with each other and a blame culture manifests. If a blame culture emerges, as it may do from time to time, it is important for senior managers to eradicate it, and exercises can be used to do this.

Organizational style is the key factor, and even within one industry there is a huge difference in organizational culture between organizations. High reliability organizations need a firmly defined organizational culture because people work very closely and are interdependent. An organization with a positive management style can imbue a team ethic. The employees of an organization with a disruptive culture may not value teamwork, and problems of communication occur because of this. The issue of in-group and out-group behaviour is important because some people, no matter what position and/or experience they have, are ostracized from the in-group – this may be due to personal chemistry, personality and the management style prevailing.

Transparency is very important with respect to assessing progress and establishing how dynamic an organization is, and how an event, however caused, affects something else and there is a chain reaction. But it may not always be appropriate in a security context. When senior managers want to implement change, they bring in people to do as they say and this creates a form of creative tension. However, if the transformational process is lacking in some respect, those in middle management may resist change as they wish to retain their power base. When change does not occur in the way expected, further tension may result, and this may end in conflict and people exiting the organization.

The agency problem is for managers, to make sure that individuals and unions use their interests as identical with, or very close to, the interests of the organization. Unions have a legitimate role to play, especially when the agency arrangement breaks down and the organization's objectives differ from the objectives of the people who they employ.

Resilience is a widely understood term and the characteristics of a resilient organization are known. Resilience can also be interpreted from the stance of an organization's cultural value system. Values can be felt or modelled without being formally defined. As regards an organization's risk appetite, several questions surface:

1. Do managers know that they are engaging in high-risk behaviour?

2. Are they realistic about what this means?

3. Do they actually want the level of risk they have?

4. How can they change the risk level if they need to? If it is a virtual organization and operates in a high-risk environment, top management may need to adjust the leadership model and if the organization is operating internationally, country specific as well as industry specific factors need to be taken into consideration. Additionally, management may need to review the standards governing the organization's actions and assess the level of compliance.

A wide variety of departments within an organization send staff to participate in exercises. Mini exercises, which are in fact a form of planned rehearsal of an incident likely to occur and which involves an evaluation of the individuals and organizations participating, the objective being to improve the performance capability of all concerned, are useful with respect to finding faults as regards what works, what works well and what does not work. The most productive exercises are those that tailor an individual's requirements to the organization's requirements, and where managers have established what the objectives of staff development represent. Training can be viewed as passing on immediate knowledge for skill enhancement and education is more broad based and linked with satisfying learning needs.

Exercises of varying degrees of complexity can be used to promote organizational learning. An exercise may be complex to write but it should model what the organization does and what people in the organization do. An exercise should not look any different to what the organization does. Security and trust can be built into an exercise, and in an exercise a person who does not have a certain security level clearance may be excluded from taking part in the exercise. However, in real life, things can go badly wrong very quickly. Hence people cannot always do what they have been told to do or go by the book/manual. An individual may need to step out side the boundary and find information quickly, and this may result in creative tension. This may be viewed as an informal approach to keeping the wheels moving, and deemed necessary in order to reduce the time taken to get people on site or equipment to where it is supposed to be. The post-exercise debriefing session will determine whether changes to policy are required or whether operating procedures need to be reviewed and/or amended.

With respect to communication, it is important to note that if an exercise is written in a formal manner it may stop some people from engaging in informal activity. A good exercise models what people do. The person in charge of the exercise is at the same time administering the exercise, observing how people actually react to situations; evaluating what they do; and noting when they do it. If handled well, and if those participating in the exercise become confident, they may perform better than expected. Hence it is crucial that the person in charge of the exercise stipulates what the exercise objectives are and what the guidelines contain.

Sometimes, if the exercise does not go the way the trainer thinks it should or has planned for it to go, then either the trainer has got something wrong or those participating in the exercise may not be doing things the way they are expected to or they may not give the trainer certain information.

Exercises can help participants to improve relationships between organizations, as explained by Lee et al. (2009: 739):

> Trust is an essential part of any cooperation between organisations or individuals. Weber (1922) described the bureaucratic organization in which individuals have 'legal' authority because they are members of a particular group (e.g., a police force) and hold an 'office' that entitles and obliges them to apply certain processes in an impersonal fashion. (As Weber said, however, these forms of authority rarely exist in their pure form – for example, the police officer may have considerable discretion in applying the law. He may apply it rigidly or in a flexible fashion based on awareness of the situation. He may see his primary role as helping

to resolve an emergency or he may see it as identifying the causes of the emergency and collecting evidence against those responsible.)

Lee et al. (2009: 740) build on this and state:

In small exercises, say within one organization, most players already know (or know of) each other. Hierarchies of position and seniority are already set. In larger exercises, however, individuals from different organizations often meet for the first time. Their initial relationship is one of deterrence-based trust, based only Weber's 'legal' authority. For instance, I may trust a police officer simply to the extent that he (or she) occupies a role in an organization that can be expected to follow certain processes. I may only partly understand the processes, but I assume that any individual in that office will apply them in the same way.

As the exercise develops, and if it is successful, this trust may turn into relational trust because I come to accept that this particular police officer is reasonable, effective, and so on, and because I come to understand the reasons behind police processes. It is also important that I should feel that the police officer understands my position. (Of course, if the exercise is not successful, my trust is likely to diminish rather than grow, and this can lead to rivalry, refusal to cooperate, and competition. One of the authors took part in an exercise on an airport where the airport fire service instructed the airport security staff to refuse admittance to the local fire service crew who were coming to back them up, as was required by the airport response plan. The reason appears to have been professional rivalry between the officers in charge. Sadly, this incident was politely ignored in the post exercise discussions, since everyone knew the personalities concerned, but its effect on trust between two organizations that should have worked together can readily be imagined. If a real incident occurred, this infantile behavior during training might lead directly to death or serious injury.)

6.2   A Review and Reflection of Organizational Learning

6.2.1   RESULTS OF THE QUESTIONNAIRE SURVEY

A questionnaire (see Appendix 1) entitled 'Exercises and Simulations of IT Systems' was distributed to a range of experts on five separate occasions. For example, the questionnaire was distributed on three occasions at Birkbeck (response rate was 4 out of 16 (the second workshop); 4 out of 20 (TSB-CAMIS Conference); and 1 out of 1 (in-depth interview with an industry expert) representing an overall response rate of 24 per cent. Although a higher number of people attended both the workshops and the TSB-CAMIS conference, some people attended both events and were not required to complete the questionnaire more than once and some people considered that the questionnaire was not relevant to their current role in the organization they worked for. One batch of the questionnaire was distributed to seven people attending a workshop at Cranfield University/Shrivenham and all seven people completed the questionnaire (100 per cent response rate). One batch of the questionnaire was distributed to 11 people attending a workshop in Brussels and four people completed and returned the questionnaire representing a response rate of 36 per cent. A summary of the results appears below.

6.2.2 SUMMARY OF RESULTS

- It is encouraging to note that 40 per cent of the respondents answered that they had participated in an IT systems related exercise within the past six months.

- Ten people or 50 per cent of the respondents took part in a total of 86 exercises, however, one person had participated in 70 or 81 per cent of the exercises and another person took part in 9 or 11 per cent of the exercises. In other words, two people accounted for 92 per cent of the participation.

- Nine people or 45 per cent indicated that the number of exercises they participated in was about right and seven people or 35 per cent indicated too few.

- With respect to how many of the exercises were organized by their own company, one person answered all, one person answered 65, three people answered 2 and four people answered 1.

- One person answered that 3 exercises had been organized by, or jointly with, another body and one person indicated 5. Two people named the type of organization: one person cited a defence organization and one person cited the FSA (Financial Services Agency) UK.

- With respect to the use of table-top exercises, one person indicated 60, one person indicated 6, four people indicted 2, one person indicated 3 and four people indicted 1.

- With respect to the use of Simulations, one person indicted 3 and one person indicted 5. The combined score of the two respondents represents 8 or 73 per cent of the total.

- With respect to the use of Live exercises, two people accounted for 8 or 89 per cent of the total. For example, one person stated 3 and the other stated 5.

- It is good to report that 16 or 80 per cent of the respondents believed that their organization had a clearly defined programme of exercises carried out at different levels.

- In response to the question: Who writes exercises in your organization? Five people indicted external consultants; four people said different people each time; three people said IT/systems; and two people stated security.

- As regards who approves exercises in the organization, as expected, senior management, security and IT/systems featured predominantly. It can also be suggested that different people are involved at different times in the approval process.

- As regards those that attend exercise planning meetings in the organization: nine people indicated security; five people indicated IT; four people indicated systems; four people indicated safety; and also external consultants and different people at specific times featured strongly.

- It was clear that senior people (management) and/or a committee (which includes senior people) approve exercises in the respondents' organization and also, security staff had a key role in the approval process.

- When exercises are shared between the respondent's organization and others, designated staff actually write/arrange them using meetings (14 or 70 per cent), letters (8 or 40 per cent), e-mail (7 or 35 per cent) and the telephone (7 or 35 per cent).

- A range of people and work practices were cited with respect to the writing and arranging of the exercises. Individuals, groups, the use of documents and the co-operative process were all cited.

- As regards who assumes responsibility for writing the exercises/ people contributing to the writing of the exercises, it is clear that a range of people are involved and that teamwork is very important and features strongly.

- It is interesting to note that 9 or 45 per cent of the respondents indicated that it is normal practice to share the writing of the exercises between staff in different organizations.

- The majority, 10 or 50 per cent of the respondents were from government and 6 people or 30 per cent were from the private sector. Two academics were represented in the population.

- With respect to the sector that the respondents' organization operated in, there was a wide coverage of sectors: services/ professional was cited mostly (50 per cent), followed by security/ defence (45 per cent), IT (40 per cent), energy (35 per cent) and Telecomms (30 per cent).

- Most of the participants (12 or 60 per cent) worked for a British/UK organization; four or 20 per cent worked for a European organization and three or 15 per cent worked for an Omani organization.

- The main benefits of exercises were judged to be: awareness, co-operation of staff across functions and learning to improve continuously (11 or 55 per cent) and four people or 20 per cent said Testing processes and procedures in order to formulate and adapt policy.

- The easiest part of the exercise to write were scenario planning or outlining the broad scenario (six people or 30 per cent) and setting up a planning group (five people or 25 per cent).

- The most difficult aspects of the exercise to write were the scenario(s) in the sense that to agree on a scenario and its planning, which was pleasing to everybody (four or 20 per cent) and taking balance to ensure an appropriate level of activities involved were delivered on time to a wide scale (four or 20 per cent).

- Many factors were cited with respect to the most worrying part of writing an exercise, including implementing lessons identified from the exercise and getting people to participate due to time pressure.

- With respect to making the processes relating to choosing and writing scenarios easier and simpler, as regards the use of injects, it was suggested that flowcharts could be considered important.

- As regards the use of briefing material, which made the process easier and simpler with respect to choosing and writing scenarios, making the scenario as realistic as possible or ensuring that real incidents were used were considered beneficial and enhanced the learning process.

- As regards the use of clearing injects and briefing material with other interested people, in the context of making the process easier and simpler with respect to choosing and writing scenarios, five people or 25 per cent answered meetings proved valuable.

- With respect to getting people to take part, which made the process easier and simpler with respect to choosing and writing scenarios, three people said relationships were important; two respondents identified meetings as important; and two respondents indicated that sector/role specific was important.

- With respect to setting a date that suits everyone, which made the process easier and simpler vis-à-vis choosing and writing scenarios, three people stated six months' warning should be given, and two people said the use of an e-mail calendar was appropriate.

- As regards negotiating with other organizations that are (or might be) involved, which made the process easier and simpler with respect to choosing and writing scenarios, a whole range of advice was offered such as: planning effectively and using external organizations; using e-mail and monitoring; using public relations more widely; holding regular meetings; involving a senior stakeholder; and interacting with co-ordinating groups. The conclusion that can be drawn is that planning is essential and continuous, and that promotional work reinforces the exercise process and ultimately acceptance of its outcome.

As can be noted from the response from the questionnaire survey, the main benefits of exercises are increasing awareness, co-operation of staff across functions and learning to improve continuously, and testing processes and procedures in order to formulate and adapt policy. With this in mind it can be suggested that training in the form of exercising helps to eradicate a number of deficiencies by highlighting and reducing the knowledge gaps of individuals.

The findings from the questionnaire survey are interesting and provide insights into various aspects of organizational learning. It can be suggested that the organizational culture that can best deal with cyber attacks, is one that supports transparency and open, interactive communication. However, it should be noted that some issues, placed in a security context, cannot be made known to a wider audience and in specific situations, the 'need to know basis' doctrine will hold true as only a privileged few are briefed/supplied with the information. The reason for this is that when attacks originate, people in the organization need to act quickly in order to repulse the attack or isolate the damage or stop the problem from intensifying.

6.3 Discussion

An issue concerning senior managers is how an industry is policed/regulated and what form of co-operation exists within the industry. It is highly unlikely that in a key industry competitors do not talk with each other or share information of a non-sensitive type; however, when somebody leaves the organization (possibly after many years' service) their expertise and knowledge is lost. This is very important with respect to a manager knowing what should be done in a certain situation when a specific incident occurs. A crucial component of training would be to ensure that there are backup information sources or staff newly appointed to a position of responsibility have access to a senior person or internal expert who can provide them with necessary expertise or advice as to where to obtain help and assistance in times of crisis. Through skill enhancement, it can be suggested that training does in part contribute to the development of an organization's knowledge base and that an example of good training is when staff are provided with the skill needed to write security policy, work with colleagues on the development of security systems, and are able to use their judgement and make rational decisions when necessary. Training can make people more confident to test their decision-making capability during role plays and it can prepare people well to use virtual training systems in order to work out their own deficiencies and knowledge gaps.

At some point in a crisis individuals will be required to use their initiative and to make decisions which are not straight from the textbook or training manual. This underscores the link between education and training in the sense that preparing a person to take responsibility for their decisions may include them attending a course of study where their knowledge is tested at the end of the course (a formal written test for example) or it may require a project report (in which case the individual is placed in a real learning environment and asked to evaluate the outcome) or it may be a multiple choice test where the individual has to answer as many questions as possible in a specific time period with little or no room for error. It can be noted, from the questionnaire analysis, that the easiest part of an exercise to write is the scenario planning element or outlining the broad scenario and also, setting up a planning group. Why it is important to highlight these factors is because they are important elements of knowledge capability building from both an organizational and individual perspective. If harnessed correctly, the cognitive powers of employees will be increased and so too will the strategic decision-making capability of the organization. This is achieved through the process of 'creative tension' and gets people to strive to achieve higher levels of attainment.

If a criminal is determined to find a way to obtain information then it may only be a question of time before an attack manifests in some way. Once this happens the key is to limit the damage. This would seem a plausible requirement that governance demands. As regards the overall standard of risk management and internal control within a company, the board must take responsibility for 'regular and systematic assessment of the risks facing the business and the values embedding risk management and internal control systems within business processes' (Financial Reporting Council 2005: 1). Internal control is necessary as it 'contributes to safeguarding the shareholders' investment and the company's assets' and allows for reliability in internal and external reporting, and can be considered influential with respect to ensuring that there is compliance with laws and regulations (Financial Reporting Council 2005: 2). It is also acknowledged that preventing and detecting fraud is possible with effective financial controls and in a changing environment, risk can be managed and controlled more effectively (Financial Reporting Council 2005: 2).

Other issues which are important are the size of the organization and the amount of risk (known as risk appetite) that the organization is able or willing to accept. For example, large companies are able to draw on various resources (both in terms of personnel and finance), whereas small companies are limited to the expertise of the sometimes over-stretched directors that are undertaking more than one task at any one time. External advice is available but is often expensive and not always company or industry specific, and in the case of small companies, timing and the time available to commission research is an important consideration owing to the fact that a long-term strategy may span six months only. Referring again to the questionnaire results, a number of key points emerged with respect to who writes exercises; the levels at which exercises are carried out; and the number of exercises engaged in. For example, in response to the question: Who writes exercises in your organization? Five people indicted external consultants; four people said different people each time; three people said IT/systems; and two people stated security. Eighty per cent of the respondents believed that their organization had a clearly defined programme of exercises carried out at different levels; and 45 per cent of the respondents indicated that the number of exercises they participated in was about right. However, as regards the latter, 35 per cent of the respondents considered that the number of exercises they participate in was too few. No doubt, there is a correlation between the size of an organization and the amount spent or invested in exercises, and furthermore, if top management do not authorize an adequate number of training exercises, the ability of the organization to become a learning organization may be affected.

The type of business model in use, and a company may operate more than one, is also an important factor in establishing how top management can implement change and ensure that all the employees understand and agree with it. Information provided by the respondents that completed the questionnaire, suggests that senior people (management) and/or a committee (which includes senior people) approve exercises in an organization and also, security staff feature highly. As regards those that attend planning meetings: the respondents indicated security, IT, systems, and safety; and the use of external consultants and different people at specific times emerged strongly. From this it can be deduced that senior managers have a key role to play in developing and nurturing a learning culture, which includes managing change in a proactive manner.

It is useful at this point to cite the work of Argyris (1996: 25), who suggests that in order to understand the context and meanings associated with the behavioural strategies of individuals, it is necessary to have an idea of how to predict certain behavioural outcomes and to understand why individuals that hold espoused theories (known as a theory of effective action), act in what can be termed an unaware manner and thus introduce discrepancies. Argyris (1996: 25) suggests that such unawareness is designed and so too is the incongruence, and as a result individuals have a theory of action 'that they use to produce all these difficulties'. This is referred to as 'theory-in-use', and the key point to note is that a full understanding of the theory-in-use mentality will allow trainers and educationalists to understand, predict, explain and change a person's behaviour or at least modify it, hopefully for the better. Other factors that need to be taken into consideration are how individuals divulge information or withhold information, and how they manipulate matters based on personal prejudice and their own perception of what is right or wrong behaviour. The situation is made more complex when power struggles break out between people in the same organization and although this may be viewed positively as it represents a form of creative tension, it needs to be borne in mind that internal conflict can increase the level of risk that the organization is exposed to and may if it goes on too long be counterproductive.

If the board of directors are not interested in improving security (owing to the cost involved) or lack the will to do it (they consider that the organization is a low threat possibility or an attack would not have much impact on the organization's ability to carry out transactions), then they may not be inclined to demand that training against cyber attacks is worth investing in. What is crucial is for both internal and external audits to be undertaken so that the organization is appraised and staff know what the situation (lack of competitiveness or low investment in IT security for example). A thorough and well conceived audit that highlights a lack of investment in IT security, would be a powerful weapon in its own right vis-à-vis raising awareness of the organization's ability to withstand a certain attack (especially a low probability, high impact attack). Such an audit would also indicate what management need to do in order to reconfigure the organization (add a security department) and implement a situational analysis so that threats can be identified and areas of vulnerability made safe. Should areas of vulnerability be identified, it is important that action is taken to increase awareness and reduce the likelihood that a destabilizing impact will occur. Compliance, in the context of adhering to the recommendations made by Turnbull (Financial Reporting Council 2005) and the guidance provided in the Information Security Management System standard known as BS ISO/IEC 27002: 2005/BS 7799-1:2005 (British Standards Institute 2007) should allow senior managers to deal effectively with assessing security risks and finding workable solutions that result in sustainability of the organization through time.

6.4   Conclusion

Many of the activities relating to training and putting systems in place to counteract actual threats can be grouped in the area of information management and systems. Reflecting on the above, it can be suggested that what is required is a risk assessment that allows senior management to make a sensible decision vis-à-vis the implementation of a cyber security strategy. It has to be said however, that guarding against or thinking about a low probability, high impact attack may not be management's highest priority.

References

Argyris, C. 1996. *On Organizational Learning*. Oxford: Blackwell Publishers.

British Standards Institute. 2007. *Information Technology: Security Technologies – Code of Practice for Information Security Management*. London: British Standards Institute.

Financial Reporting Council. 2005. *Internal Control: Revised Guidance for Directors on the Combined Code.* (October). London: Financial Reporting Council. Available at: (http://www.frc.org.uk/documents/pagemanager/frc/Revised%20Turnbull%20Guidance%20October%202005.pdf [accessed: 24 November 2010].

Lee, Y-I., Trim, P.R.J., Upton, J. and Upton, D. 2009. Large emergency response exercises: Qualitative characteristics – a survey. *Simulation & Gaming*, 40 (6), 726–51.

Weber, M. 1922. Wirtschaft und Gesellschaft, in *Sociological Perspectives*, edited by K. Thompson and J. Tunstall. Harmondsworth: Penguin (Published 1981).

Appendix 1

Questionnaire: Exercises and Simulations of IT Systems

Exercises (sometimes called simulations or drills) are used to test business continuity plans, emergency response plans, and crisis management plans, and also to test system failures.

Please answer, by providing a yes or no and/or a brief write-up, the questions listed below as accurately as you can. Do not spend time researching the details – approximations will do.

1. Approximately when did you last take part in an IT systems related exercise?

2. How many such exercises have you been involved in this year?

3. In your view was this number of exercises:

   About right   Too many   Too few   Comments

4. How many were:

   a) Organized by your company/organization?

   b) Organized by, or jointly with, another body? (Which?)

5.   How many were:

   a) Tabletops (i.e., just a discussion around a table).

   b) Simulations (i.e., a scenario with role-players).

   c) Live exercises (in which your systems were taken offline OR actual events were enacted on the ground such as a fire or major spill).

6.   Does your organization have a clearly defined programme of exercises carried out at different levels?

7.   Who writes exercises in your organization?

No one	PR	Safety/environment	Security
IT/systems	External consultants	Different people each time	Other (please) specify

8.   Who approves exercises in your organization?

No one	PR	Safety/environment	Security
IT/systems	External consultants	Different people each time	Other (please) specify

9.   Who attends exercise planning meetings in your organization?

No one	PR	Safety/environment	Security
IT/systems	External consultants	Different people each time	Other (please) specify

10. Who in senior management approves exercises in your organization?

No one	PR	Safety/environment	Security
IT/systems	External consultants	Different people each time	Other (please) specify

11. When exercises are shared between your organization and others:

a) How do designated staff actually write/arrange them?

Meetings	Telephone	E-mail/letter	Other (please) specify

b) How is the work of writing and arranging the exercise divided up?

c) Does one person take responsibility for writing them or do other people contribute to the writing of the exercises?

d) Is it normal practice to share the writing of the exercises between staff in different organizations?

12. Is your organization:

a) Government

b) Industry/private

i.   Small

ii.   Medium

iii. Large

c) An academic institution

d) Other (please specify)

13. In what sector does your organization operate (tick all that are appropriate)?

a) Telecomms?

b) IT?

c) Services/professional?

d) Security/defence?

e) Energy?

f) Other (please specify)

14. What is the nationality of your organization?

15.   What do you see as the main benefits of exercises?

16.   If you were asked to write an exercise, what would be:

a)   The easiest part?

b)   The most difficult part?

c)   The most worrying part?

17.   How do you think the following processes might be made easier and simpler when choosing and writing scenarios?

a)   Writing injects?

b)   Providing briefing material?

c)   Clearing injects and briefing material with other interested people?

d)   Getting people to take part?

e)   Setting a date that suits everyone?

f)   Negotiating with other organizations that are (or might be) involved?

Thank you for completing the questionnaire. Please ensure that you have answered all the questions set and, if you would like to receive a summary of the results, please add your e-mail address and name here:

Please return the questionnaire to:

Dr Peter Trim
Department of Management
School of Business, Economics and Informatics
Birkbeck
University of London
Malet Street
London WC1X 7HX

7

Critical Information Infrastructure Road Map

7.0   Introduction

The first workshop was held at Birkbeck College on 15 January 2010, to consider the stakeholders in a Critical Information Infrastructure Protection (CIIP) incident. It produced some excellent data that was used to produce a critical information infrastructure road map. In order to collect data, a table-top exercise process was used, which focused on interactions during two scenarios, between stakeholders represented at the meeting. We believe the workshop demonstrated that participation in this process was valuable for those who took part as they were able to take various insights back to their workplace. This chapter also contains information derived from the research project, which is of a more theoretical nature and represents an analysis of the stakeholders.

A 'road map' of stakeholders was circulated before the workshop took place and acted as a framework for discussion. Several changes were suggested and have been incorporated. The short names given to each category of stakeholder are expanded in this chapter.

The table-top exercises were used to work through two scenarios, in order to see how the participants might interact. We focused on three sorts of interaction:

- Information flow: Formal and informal systems were raised during the exercises and their characteristics are briefly compared. Some information flows modelled during the exercise are shown on the 'road map'.

- Advice and help: Assistance varies. At one extreme, the assisting organization may take full responsibility for managing an incident and recovering a system; at the other, only general advice may be offered. Types of assistance are compared and those modelled during the exercises shown on the 'road map'.

- Formal responsibility: Again, this varies, from full contractual responsibility for all or part of a system, to no, or only 'moral', responsibility. This is once again shown using the 'road map'. Some implications of formal and legal responsibility are discussed.

- Exercises offer a very constructive way forward in identifying, developing and integrating the stakeholder community.

The chapter is composed of the following: changes to the 'road map' (Section 7.1); an indication as to who the stakeholders are during a CIIP incident (Section 7.2); interactions – information flow (Section 7.3); providing assistance or advice (Section 7.4) and responsibility for maintaining systems (Section 7.5). In addition, there is a road map and the way forward (Section 7.6). Several annexes are included. Annex 1 contains a list of acronyms; Annex 2 contains a short note on an incident which took place at the time of the workshop and which provides an interesting case study of how information about a particular issue may be disseminated, and two scenarios used in the workshop are featured in Annex 3.

It is important to point out that the workshop was based on a draft 'road map' of 'stakeholders' in a CIIP incident, taking stakeholders to mean anyone who had a possible role in reacting to the incident and solving it. ('End-users', such as the public, were left out for the sake of brevity.) The workshop used two 'table-top' exercises to explore interactions between stakeholders. The scenarios used in the two exercises were:

- A virus similar to SQL Slammer affecting several UK organizations;

- A complex attack by a foreign power on UK energy industry systems, using a phishing/malware attack (based on Ghostnet, but assumed to have affected SCADA systems as well).

Although this chapter focuses on an analysis of the stakeholders in CIIP incidents and their interactions, we believe that the main benefit of the workshop was that it brought participants together in these two exercises. This exercise process enabled them to explore their expectations of each other and to consider their own organizational reactions. The UK Cyber Security Strategy (Cabinet Office 2009: 10) states:

> *Close engagement to strengthen existing cross-cutting private sector partnerships, and form new ones where required, will be fundamental to the current and longer term success of this Strategy.*

We believe that joint exercising offers a convenient facility for such 'close engagement': the exercise process is a highly efficient way of bringing about better understandings between stakeholders in this field, and we felt that the workshop demonstrated this belief. The rest of this chapter is, in a sense, secondary.

7.1   Changes to the 'Road Map'

The draft road map was broadly accepted as realistic, but several changes were proposed and have been made in the revised version used throughout this chapter.

1. Added '15–20 CERTs' (Computer Emergency Response Teams).

2. Added 'multiple ISPs' (to reflect the fact that ISPs are a major source of help and advice for each other).

3. Added police bodies, e.g., ACPO, SOCA, to show the police as responders, as well as users.

4. Added '[sponsoring] gov[ernmen]t dep[artmen]ts', e.g., Energy.

5. Altered 'police' and 'emergency services' to read LRF ('local resilience fora').

6. 'Other governments' also to include bodies such as ENISA and NATO.

In the rest of this chapter, we have tried to use the road map to show three sets of interactions. Please note that we have not tried to show all possible interactions, only those mentioned during discussion of the scenarios. The map is not a complete list of what any organization does!

7.2   Who are the Stakeholders During a CIIP Incident?

It was also possible to expand and clarify some of the terms used in the 'Road Map'.

1.   Analysts: academic or other experts on CIIP threats, e.g., Bruce Schneier (http://www.schneier.com/) or British Computer Society Information Security Specialist Group (http://www.bcs-issg.org. uk/index.html).

2.   Monitors: organizations which monitor threats, e.g., on the internet, or which aggregate and publish information about them, e.g., The Register (see http://www.theregister.co.uk/, or Internet traffic report http://www.internettrafficreport.com/).

3.   Security system vendors, e.g., Symantec/Norton.

4.   CESG (Communications Electronic Security Group): (see http:// www.cesg.gov.uk/about_us/index.shtml):

> *CESG aims to protect and promote the vital interests of the UK by providing advice and assistance on the security of communications and electronic data. We deliver information assurance policy, services and advice that government and other customers need to protect vital information services. We work on a cost recovery basis for all customer-specific solutions and services, though IA policy and Guidance documentation is usually free of charge to the UK official community.*

5.   CSOC (now being set up):

> *A Cyber Security Operations Centre (CSOC ... will bring together existing functions: to actively monitor the health of cyber space and co-ordinate incident response; to enable better understanding of attacks against UK networks and users; and to provide better advice and information about the risks to business and the public (see Cabinet Office 2009. Available at: www.cabinetoffice.gov.uk/reports/cyber_ security.aspx).*

6.   OCS:

>   *An Office of Cyber Security (OCS) to provide strategic leadership for and coherence across Government. The OCS will establish and oversee a cross-government programme to address priority areas in pursuit of the UK's strategic cyber security objectives (see Cabinet Office 2009).*

7.   CPNI (Centre for the Protection of National Infrastructure): provides integrated security advice (combining information, personnel and physical) to the businesses and organizations which make up the national infrastructure.

8.   Other governments, and multilateral organizations (includes NATO, ENISA).

9.   Software suppliers, e.g., Microsoft, Oracle, or open source clusters such as PHP. The former often publish security announcements, and offer helplines, patches, and direct contractual support. The latter tend to work via bulletin boards and the 'user community'. (Sometimes, as with MySQL, there is a hybrid model: you can have it with or without formal support.)

10.   Hardware suppliers, e.g., Dell, Sun, IBM.

11.   Backbones: operators of major internet backbones, routers, DNS servers, IXPs such as LINX (https://www.linx.net/), etc.

12.   Regulators: e.g., OfWat, OfGen, Ofcom. Proposed new powers may require companies to report on risk assessments and emergency planning, and to require companies to test emergency plans and participate in planning exercises. (Or proposed extension of CCA powers may require some CIIP providers to have Category 2 responder status.) It is also worth noting that safety regulators (e.g., HSE, the Food Standards Agency) often impose 'fail-safe' regulations which would exacerbate the effect of a CIIP incident, by making it illegal to continue where there was any doubt about a system.

13.   Police: as both regulators and responders (including SOCA, ACPO, local resilience fora) – as well as users (see below).

14.   External ICT support (companies who offer support to users).

15.   PSTN telecoms providers (e.g., BT).

16.   Multiple ISPs (e.g., Zen, Namehog), who may manage incidents co-operatively, either through IXP agreements, or informally through personal contacts.

17.   Mobile telecoms providers (e.g., Orange, 3).

18.   In-house IT (e.g., the in-house IT department of a user company such as Deloittes). They may have considerable range and depth of skills, but often are managing services provided by external contractors.

19.   System suppliers (e.g., companies who supply complete systems to users, such as pipeline SCADA systems, or NHS database systems. Typically they also accept contractual responsibility for maintaining these systems).

20.   Data sources: independently maintained sources of data, (e.g., Google Earth, police databases, Ordinance Survey's National Topographical Database) which are widely used as part of other systems. ('Several fire services, including Greater Manchester, use Ordnance Survey data non-stop around the clock to create an information database on the positions of buildings, access routes, potential hazards and so on' – see Ordnance Survey 2000).

21.   CERTs (computer incident emergency response teams, in or outside government), aka CSIRTs, etc. There are many of these but coverage is slightly patchy and the term means different things to different organizations. Some CERTs cover a country (e.g., GovCERT), some a whole sector, some a single network (e.g., JanetCERT) and some a single organization (e.g., OxCERT.) In the latter case, these CERTs are effectively the in-house IT team. While some CERTs may see their role as co-ordinating a response, the latter may see themselves as leading a response as part of a contractually involved organization. See ENISA suggestions for baseline capabilities for a government CERT (ENISA 2009b).

22.   Users: the nine identified Critical National Infrastructure (CNI) sectors, i.e., communications, emergency services (including local

resilience fora), energy, finance, food, government, health, transport and water). Some users have set up CERTs, Information Exchanges or WARPS (lists of these were previously available at https://www. ms3i.eu/ms3i/reports/MS3i_main_Report_v3.0.pdf and http:// www.eurim.org.uk/activities/e-crime/IA_UK_Community_Map. pdf, but both these sites now appear to be defunct). In general, WARP and CERT coverage does not seem to be consistent.

ENISA (ENISA 2011) publishes a free 'who's who' directory on network and information security, which includes some corporate and academic contacts, as well as government agencies, but this only lists 17 CERTs (or CSIRTS), and no WARPs. It seems to us that the lines of communication during CIIP incidents are still very fluid. There are three models. Firstly, the 'open-source', 'self-organizing' culture is very strong, particularly for anything to do with the internet. Here people tend to be suspicious of what they may see as government regulation or intervention, and to seek their own help from a tight-knit informal circle of other experts. This is an important source for many users and suppliers. Typically, they rely on the 'user community' and have enough in-house expertise to sort out what is useful from this community and to apply it. Secondly, for many organizations, CII systems are supplied, in whole or in part, by a third party. The user may have an in-house IT division, but often does not have the expertise to solve major problems. As a result, these users will turn at once to their suppliers, who are typically commercial organizations with proprietary systems. The suppliers may not be based in the UK, which may led to problems with getting urgent help in different time zones, and their priorities may not lie with UK companies who may be only a small part of their client portfolio. In large and complex organizations there may be no single person or group who actually fully understands the corporate network and other systems, and it is quite likely that not all parts of a system are covered by third party support. Thirdly, governments and organizations are setting up a network of bodies which act to:

1. Disseminate general 'pre-incident' advice and training.

2. Obtain and disseminate information about threats or incidents as they occur. Often there is a great deal of duplication as reports from one source are picked up and repeated on news aggregators like 'The Register' and on the news services of several CERTs. (See Annex 2 for a short discussion of this process.)

3. Obtain and supply advice or help to organizations affected by incidents.

Coverage seems to be patchy: for instance, Oxford has OxCert, and the telecoms industry has NEAT – but do all universities and sectors? And do they all offer similar services and ability levels? Even when these bodies exist, their need to cover a wider range of clients may mean that the help they offer is diluted for any individual organizations. There is a fourth set of stakeholders which has a more general interest in maintaining CII, and which we did not analyse in depth. These include:

1. The public.

2. Organizations such as the police or Financial Services Authority, who may need to take a broad view of an incident to establish whether a crime is being committed, and if so to investigate it.

3. Government, which has a broad responsibility not only to protect its own operations but also to ensure that 'UK Ltd' continues to operate normally. This involves 'sponsoring departments' such as the Department of Energy, as well as specific CIIP agencies like CPNI.

7.3   Interactions 1: Information Flow

In the two scenarios we discussed, it was clear that there would be two notification channels by which users or suppliers who had experienced an incident would notify others:

1. Formal notification (e.g., to CERTs or to CPNI/ CESG), often through government-mediated channels.

2. Informal, e.g., ISPs or system administrators talking to each other about observed spikes in activity, or users talking to suppliers about systems which were going down.

It is clear that these two systems operate independently, but in the same space. Some UK public-sector participants, for example, did not believe that they had any obligation to report incidents to the UK government (because they might be in-house problems which should not be publicized, and because the organization was not sure to whom to report). Please see Table 7.1 and Figure 7.1.

Table 7.1   Interactions information flow

	For	Against
Formal systems (e.g., notify CPNI or CERT, or contractual) BLUE (dotted line) on road map.	Likely to cover more organizations. Information likely to be more consistent and assessed. Anyone relevant can join. Focused on alerting, may be general to cover several sectors.	May take some hours to issue a warning. Do not operate in all sectors, but where they do operate should be open to all relevant organizations. For commercial or other reasons, sources may not give full information if this is to be widely distributed. Multiplicity of formal systems may lead to confusion (e.g., numbers of CERTs).
Informal systems (e.g., system admins talking, websites) RED (continuous line) on road map.	Speed: may operate within minutes. Industry-specific. Focused on finding quick solutions 'at the sharp end': likely to be very sector specific.	May exclude some organizations which are not 'well-connected'. Information anecdotal; may vary depending on who you speak to. May not operate in all sectors. May be exclusive, for commercial reasons, or act as 'stovepipes'. Timing may be erratic as information distribution system is not optimal (e.g., individual telephone calls).

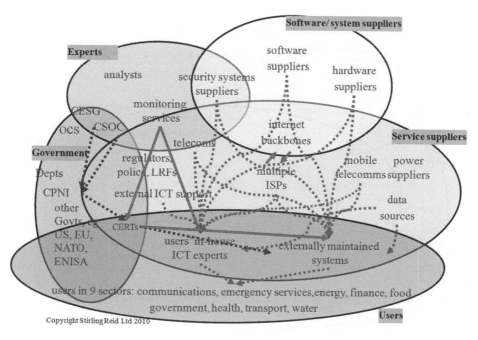

Figure 7.1   CIIP: Information flows

See Annex 2 for a brief analysis of information flow during a high profile incident which took place at the time of the workshop. This suggests that the roles of both formal and informal systems need clarification and purpose.

7.4   Interactions 2: Providing Assistance or Advice

Similarly, it is clear that there are three types of advice/assistance sources for users hit with a serious incident:

1.   Customized (typically software or system vendors or system operators who may accept full or partial responsibility for fixing an individual system).

2.   Specific (typically open source systems, CERTS, anti-virus software packages, etc., who may provide specific advice, but do not accept responsibility for implementing it).

3.   General (e.g., government bodies, CERT mailing lists such as CSIRTUK advisories, websites).

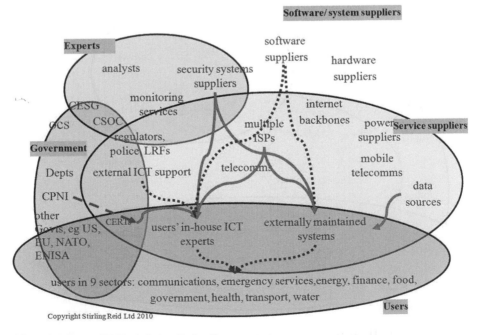

Figure 7.2   CIIP: Advice/help flows

Suppliers of anti-virus services probably fall somewhere between these two categories (see Figure 7.2 and Table 7.2).

Table 7.2   Interactions providing assistance and advice

	For	Against
First line (e.g., systems supplier). BLUE (dotted line) on road map.	May be most specific and detailed. Likely to be quick. Have organizational reputations to maintain, so have an interest in providing good rapid service to users. Strong focus on solving specific problems quickly and restoring service. May not require any expertise from user.	May be unwilling to admit failures for commercial reasons. Can cope with only their own systems: less useful if problem involves interfaces with systems provided by other organizations. May not be adequately resourced to cope. May not be able to handle very large number of requests.
Specific but not participatory (e.g., anti-virus software). RED (continuous line) on road map.	Likely to be quick. Widely available. Often updates software automatically.	Their contribution sometimes needs some user interpretation and expertise before it solves the problem. May provide inconsistent or contradictory advice. May react too quickly, and offer advice which proves to be wrong. May not be involved until system has actually gone wrong.
Third line (e.g., industry bodies, governments, web sites). PURPLE (dashed line) on road map.	May be able to balance and assess different sources of advice. May issue warnings to those not yet affected. Government may be able to shut down systems if CERT has direct access to core infrastructure like IXPs, or may have legal powers to shut down ISPs.	Provide advice but usually not specific assistance. Often get specific advice at second hand, rather than originating it themselves. Likely to be slower. May have to service a variety of users, so cannot focus on any one. May be generalized and need interpretation for specific users. In an incident involving different systems, are more likely to provide advice on the broader picture rather than a single system.

7.5   Interactions 3: Responsibility for Maintaining Systems

In parallel to the types of assistance available (see previous section) there are broadly three types of responsibility taken by any one organization for helping any other during an incident:

1. Formal, e.g., if a system supplier is contracted to maintain the operations of a system at all times, and the user only operates it. (An example might be an NHS database.) Typically this should involve a service-level agreement (SLA), though sometimes it does not, and sometimes even when it does, the SLA is of doubtful value. Ideally this type of support is total, i.e., the user simply hands the whole problem over to the help provider. Typically the help provider, when accepting the system, may rely on its own network of partial or informal support providers. (See below.)

2. Partly formal, when the help supplier has a responsibility to support part of a system (e.g., Microsoft may supply MS SQL to run an NHS database, and may have a support contract under which they will advise on how to recover a damaged SQL database; but they do not have responsibility for the overall operation of a system which may also involve other software and communications). The user may have to contact several support providers, and balance the advice of one against the others.

3. None or informal, e.g., when the source of advice or help has no contractual relationship with the affected user. Examples would be the CPNI and other government bodies, and many CERTs, which have a moral obligation to provide accurate help, but are not contractually liable if they fail to do so. Their support is likely to be more generalized and at one remove. (For example, they may supply information about a SQL injection attack, but cannot advise on how to rewrite a particular software package to prevent this attack from succeeding, or how to recover a damaged SQL database.) The user must do most of the work.

Incidentally, it is a feature of many SLAs that the compensation for failing to meet the agreed service level is rarely compatible with the loss to the user. For example, a company which has lost significant market share owing to a lengthy failure of its accounting, sales and logistics database is unlikely to be fully compensated by a refund of the fees paid to the database system provider. In this sense, final responsibility to satisfy its own clients rests largely with each organization, at each link of the chain. (The UK Cyber Security Strategy refers to the need for 'the encouragement of standards and ... to refine procurement' – Cabinet Office 2009.)

It is also the case, particularly in regulated industries, that faults or system vulnerabilities could breach legal obligations, and lead to penalties against a company. There is therefore a disincentive to report them, since this may lead to allegations that the user itself has not lived up to its responsibility, and result in subsequent fines or limitations on permission to operate. Even in a strongly ethical company, corporate lawyers would almost certainly advise against any over-early reporting which could reach government ears. Please see Table 7.3 and Figure 7.3.

Table 7.3   Interactions: Responsibility for maintaining systems

	For	**Against**
Formal (e.g. SLA*, contractual) RED (continuous line) on road map.	Defined expectations and service levels set out. Defined routes for seeking and giving help set out and hopefully exercised. Help likely to be specific and targeted. If well done, likely to provide the fastest solution and most targeted/usable solution.	SLAs only of limited use if not properly backed up and tested. May provide a false sense of security. Contractual agreements lead to litigation, reluctance to incur liability, tendency to cast blame elsewhere, rather than objective analysis. If a single organization is responsible for providing help, it may not have adequate skills or resources, and may not seek external help. Organizations involved may be unwilling to share information about the issue if it would damage organization's reputation. Only available to limited range of users.
Partially formal (e.g. SLA for part of an operation) BLUE (dotted line) on road map.	Defined expectations and service levels set out for some aspect of the user's needs, and defined routes for seeking and giving help set out. Help likely to be specific and targeted. If well done, likely to provide a quick, targeted, usable solution to at least part of the problem.	As above. While providing a good service for some aspects of a user's system (e.g. its hosting by an ISP), accepts no responsibility for other aspects (e.g. an ISP cannot help with non-hosting issues.) Where one or more partial service providers exist, the user may find himself falling between two stools if each seeks to claim that the other is responsible.
None or informal (e.g. industry body, CERT) PURPLE (dashed line) on road map.	Likely to be objective, with no 'axe to grind'. May have access to wider sources of expertise. Typically have contact with much wider bodies, e.g. other CERTs, and may see a wider picture if there is one.	Typically accepts no formal responsibility, offers help on a 'best efforts' basis. There are multiple sources of informal help, e.g. CERTs, software security vendors' websites. User may find it difficult to know which is best.

Table 7.3   Continued

	For	Against
None or informal (e.g. industry body, CERT) PURPLE (dashed line) on road map.	Services available even to users who have not taken out a contract with help provider.	Help may be general and need customizing before use. User needs skills to sort out what to do. Consultation/assessment process may lead to delays in issuing advice. Perceived not to share the commercial or other pressures facing their 'customers'. May be constrained by security or privacy concerns.

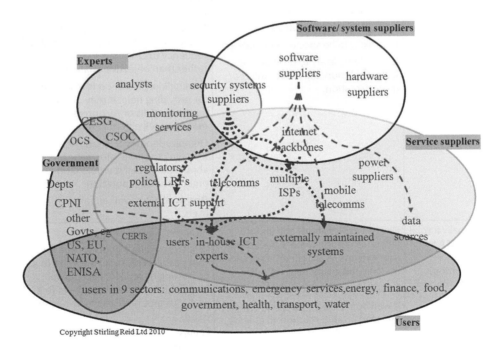

Figure 7.3   CIIP: Lines of responsibility

7.6   The Road Map and the Way Forward

This is a complex field and this short account only scratches the surface. Many different sectors are potential victims of a CIIP incident, and there are many possible types of incident and many technical infrastructures which can be at risk. For these reasons we have suggested a 'road map' of the organizations involved in CIIP, and used two table top exercises to identify some of the routes that organizations might take across the map under given circumstances. We hope that these 'road maps' at least help to clarify some of the stakeholder relationships, if only for two possible scenarios.

One benefit of exercises, whether table-tops or full-scale exercises like the 'Cyberstorm' series, is that they help to map out dynamic or uncertain relationships, by exposing them to something quite like reality. For example, the ENISA 'Good Practice Guide on National Exercises' (ENISA 2009a) identifies among others these benefits of exercises which involve multiple organizations:

- They can identify interdependencies that they may not have been aware of.

- They can practice working together with their counterparts at other organizations.

- They can share best practices in their procedures.

- They can test whether their own procedures work well in practice.

- They can test emergency contact information and channels of communications across organizations.

- They can develop trust across organizations to jointly work toward more resilient networks.

- They can demonstrate preparedness to their customers, partners, and regulators.

- It seems to us that such an exercise programme is particularly needed now, to help stakeholders in UK CIIP to sort out interdependencies, develop trust, and build on existing best practices. Many of the organizations need more publicity and resources. An additional benefit will be to help participants to build their own 'road maps' of the other stakeholders most relevant to themselves, and to improve mutual understanding and expectations.

One industry participant in the 2008 US-led 'Cyber Storm 2' exercise said:

Public/private partnership is easy to say, but it's very hard to do in reality ... That is why communication channels must be established, tested and kept fresh well in advance of a crisis. That includes activities as mundane as having an up-to-date list of contacts with current telephone numbers and alternate means of contact (Nicholas 2008).

Academic analysts have commented that:

General societal consensus on the need for public-private partnerships to protect critical infrastructure has not yet translated into clarity as to how such policies could be implemented under the current market system. In this context, understanding the formal boundaries that divide public and private spheres of actual operation may be less important than understanding boundaries of accountability and capability that define institutional arrangements, be they public or private. The challenge to public policy is to structure an incentive system that provides for adequate robust internal operations, functional decentralization, system redundancy, as well as public-private and private-private coordination (Pommerening 2004: 12).

Issues of co-ordination become even more difficult when many of the players in a 'British' incident are likely to be multi-nationals, and many of the implications are international. Whatever the 'top-down' policy may be, we suggest that an exercise programme can work pragmatically to build co-ordination at several levels:

1. CERTs (whether national, sector or company) should hold internal exercises, but also exercise with their 'clients' and their service providers. (So, for example, a water industry CERT should exercise with one or more utility companies, and also with a SCADA system supplier or a PSTN supplier.)

2. Individual users should exercise with their CERTs and suppliers, and also with their 'customers'. So, for example, a SCADA system supplier might exercise with its own suppliers, e.g., the PSTN or an ISP, but also with an oil company which used its systems to control a pipeline. Where software suppliers have support lines, it would sometimes be worth making calls to these as well.

3. Government should encourage exercises involving one or more CERTs, so that they can map out the territory around them: and so that both sides are more aware of what each offers and needs.

These exercises should normally be 'table-tops', but the aim should be to build up to a larger exercise, perhaps held annually for each sector.

Annex 1: Some Acronyms

ACPO: Association of Chief Police Officers
CCA: Civil Contingencies Act (2004)
CERT: Computer Emergency Response Team
CIIP: Critical Information Infrastructure Protection
CPNI: Centre for the Protection of National Infrastructure
CSIRT: Computer Security Incident Response Team
ENISA: European Network and Information Security Agency
ISP: Internet Service Provider
IXP: Internet Exchange Point
LRF: Local Resilience Forum
NATO: North Atlantic Treaty Organization
NEAT: National Emergency Alert for Telecommunications
PSTN: Public Switched Telephone Network
RAYNET: the Radio Amateurs' Emergency Network
SME: Small or Medium Enterprise
SOCA: Serious Organised Crime Agency
WARP: Warning, Advice and Reporting Point

Annex 2: How is an Alert Disseminated? A Short Case Study

The German Federal Office for Information Security (Bundesamt fuer Sicherheit in die Informationstechnik, or BSI) released a statement[1] on 15 January 2010, advising readers not to use the Microsoft Internet Explorer (IE) browser until a flaw had been patched. ('Deshalb empfiehlt das BSI, bis zum Vorliegen eine Patches von Microsoft auf einen alternativen Browser umzusteigen'.) IE is very widely used. The fact that the vulnerability was public knowledge means that attacks may well now be made using it. This was therefore a major story.

Microsoft released their own statement on 14/15 January,[2] acknowledging this vulnerability and saying that the company was working on a patch.

---

1   See https://www.bsi.bund.de/cln_156/ContentBSI/presse/Pressemitteilungen/Sicherheitsluecke_
    IE_150110.html
2   See http://www.microsoft.com/technet/security/advisory/979352.mspx

(According to some sites, the cure is very simple, i.e., set IE's security setting to 'high', though this may restrict some browsing. Just how serious this vulnerability is, is the main question for most users, and many users will not necessarily trust the Microsoft answer.)

This story also attracted attention because the German authorities were seen to be taking a stand against Microsoft. The French authorities issued a similar statement later on 15 January,[3] including the statement 'Le CERTA recommande l'utilisation d'un navigateur alternatif'. Some European governments have taken a firm stance in the past against Microsoft's inclusion of IE in Windows software, arguing that this was against EU competition legislation, and some may argue that the issue of the German and French advisories had a political motivation. (Browser software is usually free and it takes only a few minutes to change to an alternative.)

From the point of view of a UK system administrator, how would one find out about this? The story was widely covered in the specialist media, e.g., *The Register* on 15 January,[4] Computing.co.uk,[5] Sophos,[6] the IEEE Spectrum,[7] and many others. The story was also widely reported in mainstream media, e.g., Businessweek,[8] quoting Bloomberg agency, and the BBC.[9] There were at least 36 'tweets' on Twitter.[10] The story was also covered in blogs and aggregators. One of the authors' RSS feed readers turned up references in several sources, for example on Sitepoint.[11]

However, national authorities varied. There is no reference to IE in the US-CERT Vulnerability Summary for the Week of 11 January 2010 (issued on 18 January 2010),[12] but the Australian CERT put up an advisory on 15 January.[13] According to the *Daily Telegraph*[14] 'a spokesman from the British Cabinet Office

---

3   See http://www.certa.ssi.gouv.fr/site/CERTA-2010-ALE-001/index.html
4   See http://www.theregister.co.uk/2010/01/15/ie_zero_day_exploit_goes_wild/
5   See http://www.computing.co.uk/computing/news/2256285/germany-ditch-internet-explorer
6   See http://www.sophos.com/blogs/gc/g/2010/01/16/german-government-internet-explorer/
7   See http://spectrum.ieee.org/riskfactor/computing/it/avoid-microsoft-internet-explorer-german-security-agency-says
8   See http://www.businessweek.com/news/2010-01-16/germany-says-don-t-use-explorer-until-microsoft-patches-flaw.html
9   See http://news.bbc.co.uk/1/hi/technology/8463516.stm
10 See http://topsy.com/tb/www.dailymail.co.uk/sciencetech/article-1244138/Internet-Explorer-Germany-warns-using-IE-Microsoft-admits-browser-weak-link-China-Google-hacks.html
11 See http://www.sitepoint.com/blogs/2010/01/18/german-government-stop-using-ie/
12 See http://www.us-cert.gov/cas/bulletins/SB10-018.html
13 See http://www.auscert.org.au/render.html?it=12238
14 See http://www.telegraph.co.uk/technology/microsoft/7025392/UK-Government-will-not-warn-again-Internet-Explorer.html

told *The Telegraph* that the British government would not be issuing a similar warning and instead would be referring anyone who was concerned about cyber security to getsafeonline.org'. Getsafeonline offers general advice,[15] e.g., that IE 'contains many safety features', and has a specific warning (dated 18 January), which quotes the Microsoft security advisory:

> *Microsoft is investigating reports of limited, targeted attacks against customers of Internet Explorer. Investigation so far has shown that Internet Explorer 6 Service Pack 1 on Microsoft Windows 2000 Service Pack 4, and Internet Explorer 6, Internet Explorer 7 and Internet Explorer 8 on supported editions of Windows XP, Windows Server 2003, Windows Vista, Windows Server 2008, Windows 7, and Windows Server 2008 R2 are vulnerable.*

> <u>*How do I fix it?*</u> *CPNI are monitoring the situation and will publish further advice if the risks change.*

An advisory[16] was put out by CSIRTUK on 18 January (picked up at 11:49 on 19 January). This repeats the Microsoft security advisory word for word and does not add any comment. JanetCERT does not appear to cover it, at least not on the public areas of its website. Nor does OxCERT, nor the Cambridge University site,[17] nor the University of Oslo CERT[18] (its most recent news article as of 19 January was August 2009). Many other listed CERTs are private, and we could not check them.

Twenty-three WARPS are listed on the UK government site.[19] Some do not seem to be operating any longer (e.g., NHSWARP, PenWARP). The Irish WARP for SMEs is present on the web[20] but does not allow new logins, giving a software fault message when you try. Most WARPS are private (e.g. CY2 WARP, MODWARP) and either do not give an internet address, or require login.

Many private sector WARPs seem to be defunct. Of those that are accessible, examples we inspected do not refer to the IE issue – e.g., the Guild of One-Name Studies (a Yahoo group).[21] It is notable that WARP coverage is

---

15   See http://www.getsafeonline.org/nqcontent.cfm?a_id=1159
16   See http://www.cpni.gov.uk/products/alerts/3919.aspx
17   See http://ucsnews.csx.cam.ac.uk/articles/2010/1
18   See http://www2.usit.uio.no/it/cert/
19   See http://www.warp.gov.uk/Index/WARPRegister/indexcurrentwarps.htm#S3
20   See http://www.iriss.ie/iriss/
21   See http://tech.groups.yahoo.com/group/guild-warp/

very uneven – for example virtually no business sectors have WARPs, and only two voluntary organizations (including the Guild of One-Name Studies, a genealogical association which, although of interest to many, may not count as part of the UK's critical national infrastructure; the other is the RAYNET WARP, which may).

This is a very short and incomplete survey of information flow relating to one issue, and that issue is admittedly an anomalous one. However it does raise several questions. The government site on WARPs (www.warp.gov.uk) distinguishes three core services that WARPs should provide:

1.   Filtered warning services ('where members receive only the information they need').

2.   Advice brokering services (e.g., a bulletin board where members can share solutions to problems).

3.   Trusted sharing services (e.g., where they can share anonymised incident reports).

Given these objectives, we wonder:

1.   What is the role of advisories from CERTs when a story has already been covered in public media (e.g., specialist news sources such as *The Register*)?

2.   The German, French and Australian governments issued advisories, but the US and UK did not. Such decisions are made on purely technical grounds, but will other motives be ascribed to the CERT or WARP which made them? Is this a problem for the body which issued them?

3.   How might a UK SME, or UK systems owner, have heard about this story? How might they, with no specialist technical knowledge, form a judgement about the seriousness of the vulnerability, and decide what action to take?

The references relating to the above are cited below. As they almost all relate to ephemeral news items on websites, some may no longer be available.

Annex 3: Two Scenarios Used in the Workshop

Scenario One

MODULE ONE

Approximately one hour after a worm similar to SQL Slammer is released in the UK, it is reported by a US monitoring service, which sends out an alert. Two security software houses announce patches within an hour. The worm appears to exploit a previously undiscovered vulnerability in MS SQL. Microsoft initially cannot trace the vulnerability and point out that in most of the reported cases the MS SQL installation interface is with PHP software rather than Microsoft products.

A major NHS database system suffers a complete failure, affecting medical records, scheduling of operations, and diagnoses. NHS trusts respond by delaying non-urgent operations and reverting to paper records and internal contacts.

The databases of two UK telecomms operators also fail, and they are unable to maintain mobile telephone coverage. This causes local difficulties for police forces and ambulance trusts.

A large UK consultancy company is forced to close its intranet and knowledge sharing system, and its internal diary system collapses.

QUESTIONS (FOR FACILITATOR TO USE)

1. How would you (i.e., each scenario participant) expect to hear of these incidents?

2. To whom might the hospitals, telecomms companies, and consultancy company, turn for help? (That is who should they turn to, and who would they actually turn to?)

3. What agencies, vendors, or other organizations might step in to offer help?

4. Would anyone give the UK public an authoritative view of the situation?

MODULE TWO

Three hours later, the worm has spread quickly, affecting mostly MS SQL databases in the UK, some in the USA, and smaller numbers in Germany and France. The worm does appear to be limiting its spread largely to installations in the UK.

It is now confirmed that the fault is with MS SQL, rather than another product. However, there appear to be two different worms, using different codes. The two software 'fixes' being supplied by US vendors each remove only one version of the worm: using them on the wrong version has no effect.

There is a BBC news story alleging that a third version of the worm has been identified. This one has no immediately visible effect. Instead, it slowly corrupts any database to which it gains access, changing a few random numeric fields by a one random digit each time a query is run. According to the BBC story, which seems to be incorrect and based on a false rumour spreading form the US, this worm has affected MySQL as well as MS SQL installations. This report creates serious concern across the business and financial community.

There is some evidence of unusual patterns of share trading in the US and UK, affecting one large UK financial company, just before the worm was introduced.

QUESTIONS

1. After three hours, what co-operation channels between affected organizations would you expect to be established?

2. Who in the UK will be able to judge if the BBC report is wrong, and how would they reach industry (i.e. computer users) and the public (i.e. users of medical services, telecomms, etc.)? What messages will reach the stakeholder communities?

3. To whom will stakeholders turn for help/advice?

4. Does the possible criminal element introduce new stakeholders, or alter the situation for existing ones?

Scenario Two

MODULE ONE

A major oil company's UK oil product pipeline has suffered an unexplained shutdown, which it is attempting (in house and with the system vendor) to restart it. The system vendor is reassuring its client that this problem will be resolved quickly, and is consulting its overseas head office for help. The oil company believes that a shutdown lasting longer than 24 hours will lead to shortages and queues at filling stations.

A UK electricity supplier is having difficulties with its network control system, which seems to be suffering from a 'denial of service' attack, and has slowed right down. The same thing is happening to a UK academic network. (Since one is built on Windows/ MS SQL and the other on Unix/ MySQL, the administrators of each do not personally know each other, and are talking to different software security experts.)

The Police receive a report from a power generation company, alleging that their telephones are being tapped. It appears that details of a confidential meeting have been obtained by an environmental pressure group, and the company can only assume this information was leaked this way.

An ISP in the UK notices large amounts of unusual activity on some of its clients' accounts. The clients concerned are two energy trading companies.

QUESTIONS

1.   To whom would the organizations listed above report these events, if at all?

2.   Who if anyone might be in a position to speculate about a possible linkage between these incidents?

3.   Do you think there is a linkage? What might it be?

4.   Is this a national problem? Or a problem for the companies concerned to solve individually? Or is it one for software vendors to solve?

MODULE TWO

Two days later, CPNI receive an unconfirmed report from an intelligence source.

Over the last few months, the UK has taken a leading role in criticizing a major East Asian country over its allegedly poor environmental performance. According to the report, this country's intelligence agencies have set up a malware system, called 'Toastnet', which is infiltrating UK energy producers and major consumers. Their intention is to gather information about any UK environmental misdeeds, which might be used to counter criticisms made by the UK.

According to the intelligence report, the system gains access to e-mail accounts, and uses them to introduces malware which takes control of the infected machines. Unfortunately Toastnet's malware has a flaw in its code, which in some cases has gone out of control and is making very large numbers of database and file queries. The effect varies in intensity, but at its worst is similar to a DDoS attack. In other cases it has gone straight through firewalls and has infected SCADA systems, which it is overloading. In some cases, as well as reading files on infected machines, it appears to be deleting them, though it is not clear if this is intended.

The country concerned is reported to be highly embarrassed. It has stopped the attack and shut the Toastnet system down, but there are still an unknown number of infected systems where the malware is still running. The originating country has decided to deny all knowledge of the attack (so it is not prepared to provide any help clearing it up.)

HSE are questioning the safety of operating major COMAH sites when the safety management systems may not be reliable. They say it is essential to produce an audit of which sites are affected and which are not, before the UK runs out of fuels and chemical products.

QUESTIONS

1. Who makes a 'worst case' analysis of this situation?

2. How much can (or should) government share confidential information with the private sector?

3.   What are the mechanisms for co-ordinating the government response?

4.   What are the mechanisms for co-ordinating responses in each industry sector, and between government and industry?

5.   What monitoring systems are put in place to ensure that the lessons learned are available and acted upon in future (e.g., training or staff development programmes or new departments with additional expertise or enhanced internal auditing procedures etc.)?

References

Attorney-General's Department, Australian Government. 2008. *Cyber Storm II: National Cyber Security Exercise: Final Report.* Available at: http://www.ag.gov. au/www/agd/agd.nsf/Page/Publications_CyberStormII-September2008 [accessed: 31 December 2009].

Brenner, S.W. 2009. *Cyberthreats: The Emerging Fault Lines of the Nation State.* Oxford: Oxford University Press.

Cabinet Office. 2009. *Strategic Framework and Policy Statement on Improving Resilience of Critical Infrastructure to Disruption from Natural Hazards.* (Draft-October Natural Hazards Team, Civil Contingencies Secretariat). London: Cabinet Office.

CPNI. 2007. *Good Practice Guide: Process Control and SCADA Security: Guide 3. Establish Response Capabilities.* London: Centre for the Protection of National Infrastructure (CPNI). Available at: http://www.cpni.gov.uk/Docs/Guide_3_Establish_Response_Capabilities.pdf [accessed: 31 December 2009].

Cukier, K. 2005. *Critical Information Infrastructure Protection: Ensuring (and Insuring?): A Report by The Rueschlikon Conferences.* (September). Rueschlikon: Switzerland.

DIESIS. 2008a. Report on available infrastructure simulators, DIESIS Project, 2008. Available at http://www.diesis-project.eu/include/Documents/Deliverable2.3.pdf [accessed: February 2010].

DIESIS. 2008b. Masucci, V. et al. Critical Infrastructures Ontology Based Modelling and Simulation. Available at: http://www.diesis-project.eu/include/Publications/paper.pdf [accessed: February 2010].

Dobson, I. et al. 2003. A Probabilistic Loading-dependent Model of Cascading Failure and Possible Implications for Blackouts, *T Hawaii International*

Conference on System Sciences, January 2003. Available at: http://ffden-2.phys. uaf.edu/papers/dobsonHICSS03.pdf [accessed: November 2011].

Drennan, M. 2005. The human science of simulation – a robust Hermeneutics for Artificial Societies. *Journal of Artificial Societies and Social Simulation,* 8 (1), January.

EU Presidency. 2009. Conference conclusions. *European Union Ministerial Conference on Critical Information Infrastructure Protection.* Tallinn, Estonia, 27–28 April. Available at: http://www.tallinnciip.eu/doc/EU_Presidency_Conclusions_Tallinn_CIIP_Conference.pdf [accessed: 31 December 2009].

ENISA. 2009a. National Exercises Good Practice Guide. Available at: http://www.enisa.europa.eu/act/res/policies/good-practices-1/exercises/national-exercise-good-practice-guide [accessed: 28 November 2011].

ENISA. 2009b. Baseline capabilities for national/governmental CERTs. Available at: http://www.enisa.europa.eu/act/cert/support/files/baseline-capabilities-for-national-governmental-certs [accessed: November 2011].

ENISA. 2011. Who-is-Who Directory on Network and Information Security 2011. Available at: http://www.enisa.europa.eu/publications/studies/who-is-who-directory-2011 [accessed: November 2011].

Hyslop, M. 2007. *Critical Information Infrastructures: Resilience and Protection.* New York, NY: Springer.

ICE. 2009. *The State of the Nation: Defending Critical Infrastructure.* London: Institution of Civil Engineers.

Johnson, C.W. and Williams, R. 2008. Computation support for identifying safety and security related dependencies between national critical infrastructures. Available at: http://www.dcs.gla.ac.uk/~johnson/papers/IET_2008/National_Critical_Infrastructure_Final.pdf [accessed: 5 February 2010].

Lee, Y-I., Trim, P.R.J., Upton, J. and Upton, D. 2009. Large emergency-response exercises: Qualitative characteristics – A Survey. *Simulation & Gaming: An International Journal of Theory, Practice and Research,* 40 (6), 726–51.

Mackin, T.J., Darken, R. and Lewis, T.G. 2007. Managing risk in critical infrastructures using network modeling, in *Critical Infrastructure Protection: Elements of Risk: Critical Infrastructure Protection Program* (December), Arlington, VA: George Mason University School of Law.

Masucci, V., Servillo, P., Dipoppa, G. and Tofani, A. 2009. Critical infrastructures ontology based modeling and simulation. Chapter of a book. Available at: http://www.diesis-project.eu/include/Publications/paper.pdf [accessed: 31 December, 2009].

Moss, S. 2008. Alternative approaches to the empirical validation of agent-based models. *Journal of Artificial Societies and Social Simulation,* 11 (15) (January).

National Infrastructure Simulation and Analysis Center (NISAC). 2009. Available at: http://www.dhs.gov/xabout/structure/gc_1257535800821.shtm #2 [accessed: 31 December 2009].

Nicholas, P. 2008. Quoted in 'Lessons from Cyber Storm II' by W. Jackson, April 2008, in *Government Computer News*. Available at: http://gcn.com/articles/2008/04/09/lessons-from-cyber-storm-ii.aspx [accessed: November 2011].

Ordnance Survey. 2000. Major restructuring of Ordnance Survey database to enhance British mapping news release, 28 April 2000. Available at: http://www.ordnancesurvey.co.uk/oswebsite/media/news/2000/april/database.html [accessed: November 2011].

Pommerening, C. 2004. A comparison of critical information infrastructure protection in the United States and Germany: An institutional perspective. Paper presented at the *Annual Meeting of the American Political Science Association*, Chicago (2 September), 1–30. Available at: http://www.allacademic.com/meta/p60905_index.html [accessed: 10 November, 2009].

Privacy International. 2003. Silenced – the United Arab Emirates paper. Available at: http://www.privacyinternational.org/article.shtml?cmd[347]=x-347-103788 [accessed: February 2010].

Rigole, T. and Deconinck, G. 2006. A Survey on Modeling and Simulation of Interdependent Critical Infrastructures, IEEE, *3rd IEEE Benelux Young Researchers Symposium in Electrical Power Engineering*, Ghent, Belgium, 27–28 April 2006.

Rinaldi, S.M. 2004. Modeling and Simulating Critical Infrastructures and their Interdependencies. *Proceedings of the 37th Hawaii International Conference on System Sciences – 2004*, 1–8. Available at: http://www.computer.org/plugins/dl/pdf/proceedings/hicss/2004/2056/02/205620054a.pdf?template=1&loginState=1&userData=anonymous-IP%253A%253A87.80.20.41 [accessed: 31 December 2009].

Suter, M. 2007. *A Generic National Framework for Critical Information Infrastructure Protection (CIIP)*. (August). Zurich, Switzerland: Center for Security Studies.

Trim, P.R.J., Jones, N. and Brear, K. 2009. Building organisational resilience through a designed-in security management approach. *Journal of Business Continuity & Emergency Planning*, 3 (4), 345–55.

Verton, D. 2003. *Black Ice: The Invisible Threat of Cyber-Terrorism*. Emeryville, CA: McGraw-Ill/Osborne.

Willis, H.H., Lester, G. and Treverton, G.F. 2009. Information sharing for infrastructure risk management: Barriers and solutions. *Intelligence and National Security*, 24 (3), 339–65.

Wired. (2009). Internal twitter credentials used in DNS hack, redirect, 18 December 2009. Available at: http://www.wired.com/threatlevel/2009/12/twitter-hacked-redirected [accessed: February 2010].

8

The Learning Organization and Managing Change

8.0 Introduction

As dynamic shifts in the marketplace put stress upon the organization to deliver products and services that are in demand and noting that all products and services have a limited lifecycle, senior managers need to be aware that different skills are required from time to time, and commitment to organizational learning from the top down is essential if staff are to update their skill base and become more productive. This chapter pays attention to a number of highly important topics including: training, staff development and strategy implementation (Section 8.1) and the learning organization concept and organizational learning (Section 8.2). The advantages associated with international project groups are made known (Section 8.3); changing organizational attitudes and mindsets is covered (Section 8.4) and a conclusion (Section 8.5) draws the chapter to an end.

8.1 Training, Staff Development and Strategy Implementation

Today, managers are well aware of the complexities associated with managing complex organizations and are especially aware of the need to deal with unforeseen events and impacts, in a quick and appropriate manner. Managing change needs to be planned and co-ordinated, and training managers in particular must to be aware of the skills that are needed in order to manage change effectively. In order that training managers can devise courses and programmes that increase the skill base of employees so that they can become positive agents of change, it is essential that they understand how the organization's marketing objectives are linked with or to be realigned with the organization's strategic objectives. By embracing the internal marketing concept, it should be possible to run half-day security awareness seminars, which reinforce security policy objectives. Obviously, top management need to have the vision and remain committed to staff development, at all levels throughout the organization's hierarchy (Lee 2009: 181). Understanding what motivates people and getting them to perform at a higher level of competence is important and the learning organization concept can prove influential by focusing managers' minds with respect to implementing policies and strategies that ensure that the organization grows, changes direction when necessary and adapts to market situations. However, organizations at a different stage of their lifecycle or in a young and rapidly growing market may have different priorities to those that are competing in a mature and static marketplace, and because of this it is not always useful for managers to think of benchmarking against successful industry leaders/followers. Indeed, training managers should design courses and programmes to provide knowledge and skills necessary to close the capability gaps identified and ultimately, to help reposition the company in the industry in which it competes.

Appelbaum and Gallagher (2000: 49) focus attention on why top management need to have a strategic vision, by suggesting that 'training is important with respect to staff being able to close the gaps between an organization's current reality and its future transformation'. In other words, the process of transformation not only has to be managed, it has to be planned and the planning process placed in context. There is a clear need for training and for educating employees to take security seriously, and to ensure that they do not give away passwords and company data and information, which can be used by those intent on inflicting damage on the organization. What needs to be noted is that security is in fact an attitude of mind and requires a deeper understanding of what resilience is. By approaching security from a socio-cultural perspective, it is possible to suggest that it can be embedded in the organization's value system and permeate all layers within the organizational hierarchy. Furthermore, attitudinal surveys are useful with respect to establishing how satisfied a workforce is, and can be used to detect undercurrents of discontent. Training and staff development programmes can be used to provide support and reassurance, in times of uncertainty (mergers, economic downturns and new regulatory policy), and can reinforce the organization's value system.

During periods of crisis, top management may implement a restructuring programme that does much to innovate and bring about organizational change that is aimed at repositioning the organization in the industry in which it competes. Such an approach may be considered structuralist and an opposing approach, known as the reconstructivist view, put forward by Schumpeter, suggests that innovation 'is the product of the ingenuity of entrepreneurs and cannot be reproduced systematically' (Kim and Mauborgne 2005: 210). It can be argued, therefore, that managers can create their own crisis in order to simulate change and need not be imprisoned by planning cycles. Training and staff development programmes can and should be tailored to assist managers to identify gaps, and to provide staff with a basis for devising and implementing strategic plans.

As well as managers having to deal with external threats, they also need to deal with internal threats. Owing to the fact that it is not possible to predict the behaviour of employees (and non-employees (those engaged by sub-contractors for example)), it can be suggested that an internally orchestrated attack can be more damaging than an externally orchestrated attack, because the attacker is already inside the system and can, if undetected, cover their tracks and undertake further illicit acts. An insider may not just think in terms of defrauding the organization. For example, an insider may instigate acts of sabotage when they are threatened with redundancy or when a takeover by a rival organization results in their services being terminated prematurely. Monitoring employee behaviour and changes in an individual's lifestyle are not easy issues for top management to address, as there are a number of ethical considerations and legal issues to consider.

The ability of a person to deceive or continue on a path of deceiving, may be to do with their own personality and their closeness to the perceived victim. For example, Reddy (2007: 239) has indicated that deceiving may have to do with the type of communication engaged in, and the fact that cyber space provides anonymity and cover for individuals carrying out an attack in cyber space. Cyber attacks can be planned externally and executed internally, by one person or a group of people. Those that feel dissatisfied with or alienated by employment policy, may decide to take revenge on the company – steal data/information and/or delete files of data for example. Bearing this in mind, it can be suggested that the emotional state of employees needs to be monitored through time in order to gauge if people are satisfied or likely to be a threat. To guard against inside threats manifesting, top management can reinforce the need for security and ensure that the organization's value system promotes acceptable behaviour relating to the safe keeping and transfer of sensitive data and information.

8.2   The Learning Organization Concept and Organizational Learning

The concept of organizational learning has been widely interpreted but embraces the skills, knowledge and experience of employees, and integrates this within an organizational framework, which promotes self development and improvements in working practices, management systems, policies and procedures, and strategy formulation and implementation. Senge (1999: 14) states that a learning organization is 'an organization that is continually expanding its capacity to create its future' and although adaptive learning (known as survival learning) is important it 'must be joined by "generative learning" that enhances our capacity to create'. Organizational learning is, therefore, a management process, which equips employees with the knowledge and skill they need in order to undertake their duties in a systematic and logical manner, and thus improve the organization's way of doing business. However, a broader view of what organizational learning constitutes can be found in the work of Argyris (1996). For example, Argyris (1996: 8), maintains that:

> Learning is defined as occurring under two conditions. First, learning occurs when an organization achieves what it intended; that is, there is a match between its design for action and the actuality or outcome. Second, learning occurs when a mismatch between intentions and outcomes is identified and it is corrected; that is, a mismatch it turned into a match.

Argyris (1996: 8) points out that it is individuals, not the organization itself, whose behaviour result in learning and in order to have an in-depth understanding of what learning is and how it can be harnessed to change matters for the best, it is necessary for managers to think in terms of single-loop and double-loop learning. This is owing to the fact that errors will occur and when they do, the consequences need to be thought through and corrective action taken and lessons learned and acted upon. Argyris (1996: 8–9) explains this accordingly:

> Single-loop learning occurs when matches are created, or when mismatches are corrected by changing actions. Double-loop learning occurs when mismatches are corrected by first examining and altering the governing variables and then the actions. Governing variables are the preferred states that individuals strive to 'sacrifice' when they are acting. These governing variables are not the underlying beliefs or values

people espouse. They are the variables that can be inferred, by observing the action of individuals acting as agents for the organization, to drive and guide their actions ... learning may not be said to occur if someone (acting for the organization) discovers a new problem or invents a solution to a problem. Learning occurs when the invented solution is actually produced. The distinction is important because it implies that discovering problems and inventing solutions are necessary, but not sufficient conditions, for organizational learning. Organizations exist in order to act and to accomplish their intended consequences ... Single-loop learning is appropriate for the routine, repetitive issue – it helps get the everyday job done. Double-loop learning is more relevant for the complex, non-programmable issues – it assures that there will be another day in the future for the organization.

Morgan et al. (1998: 357) have elaborated further the two distinct steps associated with organizational learning: (i) adaptive learning, which embraces existing knowledge in order to improve both the quality and the efficiency of existing operations; and (ii) generative (double-loop) learning, which is the next stage of the adaptive learning process and can be viewed from a cognitive and intellectualizing stance of problem definition and solution. It is useful at this juncture to take into account the work of Herbiniak (Morgan et al. 1998: 358–9), who suggests that when considering the issue of organizational capabilities, it is useful to think in terms of utilitarian and psychological capabilities. The former deals with organizational learning in the context of strategic planning (improved managerial skills and co-ordination between functions); and the latter deals with cognitive benefits derived from management processes and systems. Organizational learning is, therefore, a means by which people in an organization (it is also relevant to think in terms of extended organizations such as a strategic alliance for example), can develop their knowledge, skills and confidence to make appropriate decisions, and at the same time influence the organization's value system. By influencing and changing the organization's value system, the management of change will be deemed as transformational and it is hoped that staff will be energized to attain better results (a higher return on investment, shorter product development times and enhanced customer care for example).

The ways in which people learn, the development and utilization of knowledge, and the benefits associated with knowledge transfer, need consideration. Lee at al. (2009: 741) state:

> *For a learning organization culture to be established, it is essential that senior managers pay attention to how individuals learn and how they develop their skill and knowledge base.*

Kolb and Kolb (2008: 9) have provided additional insights into the topic and claim that most people do not 'understand their unique way of learning' and that 'many have not thought about what learning is and about themselves as learners'. Kolb and Kolb (2008) explain that:

> *those individuals who believe that they can learn and develop have a learning self-identity. The learner faces a difficult challenge with a 'mastery response', while the person with a fixed identity is more likely to withdraw or quit. Learners embrace challenge, persist in the face of obstacles, learn from criticism, and are inspired by and learn from the success of others. The fixed identity person avoids challenge, gives up easily, avoids criticism, and feels threatened by the success of others.*

This is an important point to note by simulation designers, trainers and educators, because they need to:

> *carefully monitor the performance of the participants and provide specific de-briefings that allow those involved in the simulation exercise to reflect and better understand what experiential learning involves. By getting individuals to think in terms of the experiential learning cycle, it should be possible for individuals to think in terms of 'when a concrete experience' is enriched by reflection, given meaning by thinking, and transformed by action, the new experience created becomes richer, broader, and deeper (Kolb and Kolb 2008: 13).*

It is useful at this juncture to quote Argyris (1996: 8): 'It is individuals acting as agents of organizations who produce the behavior that leads to learning'. Bearing this in mind it can be argued that organizational learning is in fact the sum of individual learnings by members of the organization. Another point that is significant and needs attention is the style of leadership and how the organization's cultural value system (possibly through the process of transparency) encourages information sharing, group work and the reward of highly motivated individuals. These points are crucial with respect to an organization working in a fast moving industry. In such as environment, it is clear that the learning process requires that staff take responsibility for developing their skill base and at the same time become immersed in the organization's value system. Human resource management specialists need to be aware of how the business environment is changing and what skills are required, and they need to work with internal training providers to establish training and educational awareness programmes that are suitable for a wide audience (those directly employed by the organization and employees of partner organizations: suppliers, dealers and distributors, and retails for example). Taking this into account, senior managers may 'need to make a distinction between transformational leadership and transactional leadership, and take notice of the fact that a dual leadership style can be deployed in a culturally sensitive organizational environment' (Lee 2009: 181). By setting achievable organizational learning objectives, it should be possible for senior managers to create uniqueness and to ensure that through continual improvement, the organization establishes and maintains a sustainable competitive advantage (Trim and Lee 2004: 286).

Training and staff development are aspects of human resource management policy that require continual attention. For example, Trim and Lee (2007: 335) have this to say:

> *What is important is that senior managers understand that the term 'organizational learning' is all-embracing and refers to the context within which knowledge is generated, stored, transferred from one employee to another, used to devise and implement new work practices, and ultimately, is transformational, in the sense that direction is forthcoming that positions the organization in the industry within which it competes.*

> *The organizational learning concept is focused on providing managers with appropriate technical and interpersonal skills, but is has a psychological dimension as well. For example, various staff development programs can be devised that include role play activities that are aimed at confidence building. By assuming responsibility for their actions, junior managers will gain respect from their peers and make themselves known to senior managers, who then provide them with leadership positions.*

Building on the above points, Trim and Lee (2007: 335–6) indicate that senior managers need to understand:

that the concept of organizational learning can be used to bring about change and that the change process needs to be managed in an incremental and pro-active manner.

One way in which to bring about organizational change is to institutionalize the learning process and to empower people to take responsibility for their personal development. The process of institutionalizing organizational learning is complex; however, an international project group approach can be used to facilitate the transformation process, especially when it is necessary to devise new forms of market entry. What is evident is that senior managers need to think in terms of motivating junior managers to want to achieve something higher than their immediate expectations. One way that this can be done is to encourage staff to undertake continuing professional development and to adopt an entrepreneurial approach to decision-making.

By embracing the concept of organizational learning, senior managers can encourage staff lower down the hierarchy to improve their knowledge and skill base through time, and thus acquire skills that ensure that they remain employable.

With regards to the international project group approach referred to above, it can be suggested that this represents a useful way to pool knowledge from organizational members employed by a company that is operating across borders or a domestic company that has a number of partnerships with other companies (suppliers, wholesalers and retailers, for example). The way the company is configured and the type of business model that is in place, will determine the composition of the international project group members and what their objectives are. Reference to an entrepreneurial approach to decision-making also needs explanation in the sense that entrepreneurial in this context means 'creative and fit for purpose'. Taking both these points into consideration it is possible to indicate that the security plan to be implemented will be shared or defined as a joint security plan. As a result, adequate attention will be given to such issues as interoperability and having systems in place to solve company specific cyber security problems in real time.

At this stage in the proceedings it is useful to revisit the fact that different leadership models and styles exist and these give rise to different management and business models. Some critics might suggest that the stakeholder view, which according to Johnson and Scholes (1999: 61) represents the political view of strategy development and suggests that: 'strategies develop as the outcome of processes of bargaining and negotiation among powerful or external interest groups (or stakeholders)', is more appropriate today than, for example, the Agency Theory approach, which according to Douma and Schreuder (1998: 99) is 'in its simplest form ... the relationship between two people, a principal and an agent who makes decisions on behalf of the principal'. However, the resource-based view of the firm, which maintains that 'a resource can only be the basis of a competitive advantage if that resource has certain properties' (Douma and Schreuder 1998: 159), can still be considered to be relevant as it focuses management's attention on resource availability, replication, substitution and the law of competition. What is important is that senior managers develop an organizational configuration (structure and systems) that facilitates the development of knowledge and the utilization of in-house and external expertise. Reiterating the fact that organizations are confronted with crises from time to time, and management need to adopt a proactive approach to crisis management and innovate in order to find new solutions to what can be termed survival threatening situations. The solutions may embrace technology or the implementation of a new technology, and may also be deemed as revolutionary (Greiner 1967). The work of Kim (1998: 518) is useful with respect to illustrating how an organization can construct a crisis in order to focus the creative energies of its staff, as opposed to a adopting a destructive approach, to solving problems. It should be possible for senior managers to create a crisis oriented competition that is cyber specific and which can result in a solution or set of solutions being generated that can be implemented in order to make the organization more robust. One way in which an international organization can deal with survival threatening situations and increased risk, is to establish a number of international project groups, which are controlled from the centre/ headquarters, and which are task specific. An international project group may be composed of staff from inside the company only (individuals drawn from different business functions); can be in the form of a partnership arrangement (a manufacturer linked with suppliers, wholesalers and retailers for example); or in the form of a consortium (manufacturer and selected partners including university research departments).

8.3   International Project Groups

In the context of an organization operating across borders, international project groups are a means of harnessing the knowledge and expertise of people throughout an organization and more specifically can act as co-ordinating vehicles for devising ways to implement plans and strategies. Trim and Lee (2007: 337) have provided insights into what the main purpose of an international project group is:

> to work on 'secret' projects that are deemed essential to the future survival of the organization. One can think in terms of new products for existing markets, new technology for an evolving market, new technological processes that improve manufacturing capability, and new distribution arrangements that enable the organization to provide a high level of customer service (after-sales service) on entry to the market.

> The senior manager(s) responsible for the functioning of an international project group need to ensure that those given the responsibility to discuss matters in an open and frank manner, and reach the deadlines set, are able to do so. It is because of this that the concept of organizational learning needs to be thought of as a tool for facilitating the management of change, and providing future leaders.

International project groups can be used for a number of purposes and are useful with respect to building trust-based working relationships involving partnership arrangements. They can also act as a catalyst for the development of new ideas, for promoting and managing organizational change through initiatives in interoperability involving IT systems, and can facilitate the development of new management methods and decision-making styles (e.g., achieved through small team relationship building exercises and in-house project based competitions). In-house, cross-functional project-based competitions are a good means of stimulating solutions to cyber threats in the sense that various experts can be brought together to think of current and emerging cyber threats and how the organization's risk model(s) can be amended to produce countermeasures that reduce the organization's level of vulnerability.

McGahan (2004: 87) is right to suggest that senior managers need to understand change and how it affects the industry, and Charan (2001: 82) has indicated that a leader (or one could assume senior management in general) needs to listen to advice provided and have the necessary operational experience to make what can be defined as practical and workable solutions. Workable solutions highlight the need for internal fit to be achieved, and this can be reinforced through the organizational learning concept being applied to ensure that everybody in the organization is committed to what is known as continual improvement. Figure 8.1 on the following page outlines how organizational learning underpins the strategic management process. What can be noted is that by adopting the structure outlined, individual managers will find it a lot easier to seek and utilize organizational resources for enhancing training and staff development. Furthermore, by establishing a number of strategic project groups, some of which can be viewed as permanent or semi-permanent (ad hoc and with a limited life), it should be possible to ensure that once a discovery has occurred it is recognized (e.g., documented in a change of policy or manifests in the creation of a new department or method of working), and new training and staff development programmes are designed and put in place. The training and staff development programmes will take into account the skills identified as being required in order for there to be a direct match between technological outputs and human factor requirements. The main considerations were that change had to be viewed as a continuous process and the organization itself needed to be able to embrace and adapt to change.

The following example illustrates the benefits associated with establishing an international project group(s) and how the formation of strategic project groups facilitates and drives organizational learning.

IT staff in Company X decided that they needed to restrict the organization's IT outsourcing activities because of the fact that there were too many unknowns associated with the way in which information security technology and the speed at which information security technology was emerging. Senior management considered that internal IT staff had become complacent, basically as a result of expecting answers and solutions to be provided by the outsource companies that the organization did business with. There was also a balance sheet issue in the sense that whereas it had been decided that cost savings would be guaranteed through outsourcing, it was becoming obvious that knowledge gaps existed both within the organization (as a result of older staff being made redundant) and within the outsource companies, which tended to employ young staff who left the organization after a short period in order to progress their careers with other organizations. The high turnover of labour within the outsource companies resulted in there being inadequate knowledge and support services that could be drawn upon and this was causing frustration within the organization itself.

A strategic decision was made to establish an independent organization that had a research link with an internationally renowned university, the objective being to test out ideas so that technical solutions could be implemented in real time. By linking with a university department, it was felt that a range of pitfalls associated with advances in information security technology utilization could be identified and rectified before the products and services went to market. A separate marketing organization had been established to market the company's products and services to a specific client group (the customer organizations had been carefully selected based on the percentage of business won) and an account management system was put in place to ensure that the client relationships were managed appropriately.

The example illustrates that in order for organizational double-loop learning to occur, it is essential that senior management take responsibility for putting in place individuals and mechanisms that promote organizational change initiatives, and that individuals are given the power and authority to create new learning systems (Argyris 1996: 35). The work of Heron (Postle 1996: 33–4) is worth highlighting as the 'multi-modal learning approach' encompasses a *practical* mode (skills gained from actually doing something); a *conceptual* mode (the use of language – spoken, mathematical or symbolic and the ability to analyze and debate); an *imaginal* mode (the use of imagination to understand sequences, processes and situations); and an *affective* mode (encountering and direct experience which is the result of immersion in an experience). The *imaginal, conceptual* and *action* modes of learning grow out of and are dependent on the *affective* mode, which is 'the capacity to learn at an emotional level' (Postle 1996: 34).

Drawing from and building on the work of others, Kolb (1984: 27) states that: 'Knowledge is continuously derived from and tested out in the experiences of the learner' and goes on to define learning as 'the process whereby knowledge is created through the transformation of experience' (Kolb 1984: 38). Kolb (1984: 40–41) explains that 'the process of experiential learning can be described as a four-stage cycle involving four adaptive learning modes – concrete experience, reflective observation, abstract conceptualization, and active experimentation'.

Bearing the above points in mind, it can be deduced that the international project group approach is a useful means for focusing on cyber threats in the sense that various personnel (security, marketing intelligence, business intelligence, business continuity planners, financial analysis, IT support staff, strategy, organizational support and human resource management specialists) can come

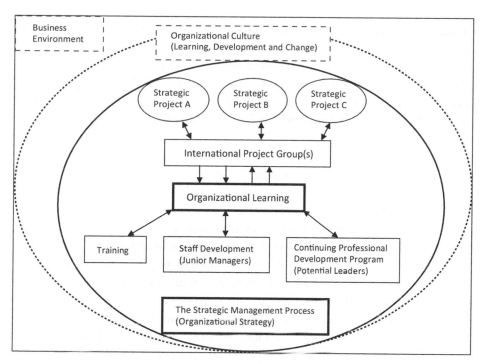

Figure 8.1   A conceptual model outlining how organizational learning underpins the strategic management process

Source: Trim and Lee 2007: 341. Reproduced with permission from Emerald Group Publishing Limited.

together with invited external specialists (CPNI, ENISA, the US Department of Homeland Security, academics and industry experts for example) to discuss the problems associated with a technology or a technological application or an evolving business model that has a greater number of interdependencies associated with it. An increased number of interdependencies may make each organization in the partnership more vulnerable to attack than was previously the case. The UK's Centre for the Protection of National Infrastructure (CPNI) is already involved in a number of Information Exchanges and these are doing much to galvanize attention towards current and emerging cyber threats on an industry basis.

Additional strategic project groups (some of which can be organized on an industry basis and others by government) will no doubt be added to the ones that exist at present and will be assigned specific tasks: to identify evolving cyber threat trends, their possible implications and necessary countermeasures; to identify the risks associated with cloud computing – private versus public provision; to identify the problems and advantages associated with outsourcing, offshoring and nearshoring; issues relating to identify theft and its ramifications for law enforcement agencies and the need for increased cross-border co-operation; the likely areas of vulnerability in supply chain configurations; and critical information infrastructure failures and the need for a relevant reputation management policy for example.

A worrying point as regards critical information infrastructure is that computer systems can be infected with viruses and data can be corrupted – this can cause malfunctions and result in terrible consequences. In the same way that a supermarket can experience somebody tampering with products and making them unsafe, banks can find that the data in their customer database has been manipulated and that unlawful financial transactions have occurred. Computer virus writing no longer requires 'rocket scientists'. Today, it is possible to purchase botnets and malware, and to unleash these on organizations and institutions or simply to hold organizations to ransom (an attack or series of attacks can stop if a certain amount of money is paid to those that are orchestrating the attack). Security analysts need to stand back and think carefully about where a potential attacker is most likely to obtain basic information, which can then be used to gain access to confidential data and information. A potential attacker may not target the company head on (try to breach a firewall for example) but may instead unleash an attack on a company via its weakest link, which may be a supplier. If a potential attacker successfully targets or 'social engineers' people in the organization's call centre, or somebody working on a help desk, they may gain unlimited access to the organization's customer accounts, and sell the data to criminals.

8.4   Changing Organizational Attitudes and Mindsets

Having the necessary information security systems in place will allow IT managers to provide greater all round protection and reduce the organization's level of vulnerability; however, training and staff development programmes will still need to be designed that are aimed at eradicating unsatisfactory aspects of human behaviour (generally poor security practice involving data handling, storage and transportation). So a case is being made for a security culture that is all embracing and which focuses attention on people's perception of what risk is and how much risk the organization can be exposed to. Having said this, it is important to note that as well as staff being concerned with all aspects of security, it is essential for other stakeholders (investors and shareholders, regulators and auditors for example) to be able to judge whether senior management have a sound appreciation of the organization's risk appetite and to balance internal and external perceptions so that the organization is not confronted with damaging publicity should a data loss arise and result in public scrutiny. A point to note is that although this is wise advice, investors in particular do not have time to second guess management on everything and take a number of issues on trust. Furthermore, the true value of information can often be best gauged if one works through a scenario that outlines what would happen if the organization's most sensitive information was lost/stolen/ altered. A scenario planning process can also help managers to establish what they are protecting and who else should be involved in the protection of the asset.

Managers are, to a certain extent, aware of the risks that the organization is facing and what is required is a sensible judgement about how to make an appropriate/effective response as an over-reaction may be just as dangerous as an under-reaction. Changing people's mindset as regards how vulnerable the organization is, can be considered a priority. It can also be said that a crisis can be the spur for initiatives and when the snow paralyzed the UK in 2009/2010, rather than have people stay at home and not work it could be that people were found an alternative method of working (remote working). Indeed, travelling to work when it is hazardous not only raises issues about whether people should be put at risk in this way but also, by working remotely, are people able to be productive? The harsh weather conditions of 2 February 2009 will be remembered for a long time as they caused major disruption to transportation in England and especially London, where all forms of transportation were effected (see http://www.guardian.co.uk/uk/2009/feb/02/snow-london-travel -chaos [accessed: 29 November 2010]). Although on a technical level the security implications associated with remote working are understood, it has to be remembered that not everybody in an organization is aware of the vulnerabilities associated with remote working and some may, because of their behaviour, place the organization or a part of it at risk. Two questions emerge: How are the potential threats prioritized? How can the benefits associated with training be quantified?

Caballero (2010: 37) suggests that managers need to focus attention on the 'weakest element in the security formula that is used to secure systems and networks', hence awareness activities and role-based training are key with respect to enhanced security. Possibly the most appropriate way to discover what the weakest element is, would be for managers to identify the risks and then for them to prioritize the risk countermeasures, and then to relate the risks back to a 'what-if' scenario and to think in terms of how the organization would recover from a low probability, high impact event. As regards security teaching methods, Caballero (2010: 38) is right to suggest that a variety of teaching methods can be used to increase the organization's skill base including lectures, case studies, workshops and hands-on practice. Senior managers can also think in terms of deploying environmental scanning techniques to provide managers with insights into how possible future events may unfold and the impact they may have on the organization. Environmental scanning is considered useful with respect to providing evidence of how the environment may change in the future and what threats may arise that cause managers to change the strategy or the mode of operation, and this should prove valuable as regards the development of an effective cyber security policy.

The following needs can be identified:

1. The organizational cultural value system needs to be underpinned by the values of senior management, and senior managers need to exhibit a proactive approach to resilience through providing guidance and leadership in all matters relating to organizational security.

2. The organizational value system needs to be transparent and flexible enough to embrace cultural change quickly, and robust enough to stop individuals misinterpreting what is required of them.

3. Open communication needs to be encouraged that reinforces the decision-making process and allows trustworthy relationships to develop, bearing in mind the fact that security often requires a degree of confidentiality.

4. A joint management decision-making approach needs to be fostered in order that partnership arrangements are viewed as trustworthy and trust-based relationships are developed that encourage information sharing when necessary.

This means establishing:

1. How technology can be used to support various forms and types of training including virtual training.

2.   How a number of separate monitoring systems, which have several objectives – to gauge employee capability as well as log and evaluate intrusions into the organization's data networks – can be used to enhance decision-making within the organization and between organizations.

3.   Evaluating how training packages can be used to enhance the decision-making process.

8.5   Conclusion

It needs to be said that protecting an organization against cyber attacks is costly, both in terms of management time and devising appropriate organizational structures, and investments in security. However, a commitment to organizational learning and a well-planned training and staff development programme can prove useful. Making staff aware of the potential problems associated with cyber attacks can be done through internal marketing and the key is to ensure that employees act in a responsible manner in order not to place the organization at risk. The following points can be noted:

1.   Being committed to organizational learning allows managers to develop an organizational culture that can continuously improve the business model that is in being, and which promotes training and staff development.

2.   A commitment from management that the organizational cultural value system will promote and nurture trust-based relationships.

3.   Organizational learning forces managers to think in terms of an organization's ability to learn though harnessing strategic intelligence.

4.   Organizations that 'learn' will enhance their strategic capability as well as their ability to respond sensibly to crises.

References

Appelbaum, R.S. and Gallagher, J. 2000. The competitive advantage of organizational learning. *Journal of Workplace Learning: Employee Counselling Today*, 12 (2), 40–56.

Argyris, C. 1996. *On Organizational Learning.* Oxford: Blackwell Publishers.

Caballero, A. 2010. Information security essentials for IT managers: Protecting mission-critical systems, in *Managing Information Security,* edited by J.A. Vacca. Burlington, MA: Elsevier, 1–46.

Charan, R. 2001. Conquering a culture of indecision. *Harvard Business Review,* 79 (4), 75–82.

Douma, S. and Schreuder, H. 1998. *Economic Approaches to Organizations.* Hemel Hempstead: Prentice Hall Europe.

Greiner, L. 1967. Patterns of organization change. *Harvard Business Review,* 45 (3), May–June, 119–30.

Johnson, G. and Scholes, K. 1999. *Exploring Corporate Strategy: Text and Cases.* Hemel Hempstead: Prentice Hall Europe.

Kim, L. 1998. Crisis construction and organizational learning: Capability building in catching-up at Hyundai Motor. *Organization Science* 9 (4), 506–21.

Kim, W.C. and Mauborgne, R. 2005. *Blue Ocean Strategy: How to Create Uncontested Market Space and Make the Competition Irrelevant.* Boston, MA: Harvard Business School Press.

Kolb, D.A. 1984. *Experiential Learning: Experience as the Source of Learning and Development.* Upper Saddle River, NJ: Prentice Hall, Inc.

Kolb, A.Y. and Kolb, D.A. 2008. The learning way: Meta-cognitive aspects of experiential learning. *Simulation & Gaming* OnlineFirst on 10 October as doi: 10.1177/10468781083225713 [accessed: 20 October 2008].

Lee, Y-I. 2009. Strategic transformational management in the context of inter-organizational and intra-organizational partnership development, in *Strategizing Resilience and Reducing Vulnerability,* edited by P.R.J. Trim and J. Caravelli. New York, NY: Nova Science Publishers, Inc., 181–96.

Lee, Y-I., Trim, P.R.J., Upton, J. and Upton, D. 2009. Large emergency response exercises: Qualitative characteristics – a survey. *Simulation & Gaming,* 40 (6), 726–51.

McGahan, A.M. 2004. How industries change. *Harvard Business Review,* 82 (10), 87–94.

Morgan, R.E., Katsikeas, C.S. and K.A. Adu. 1998. Market orientation and organizational learning capabilities. *Journal of Marketing Management,* 14, 353–81.

Postle, D. 1996. Putting the heart back into learning, in *Using Experience for Learning,* edited by D. Boud et al. Buckingham: The Society for Research into Higher Education and the Open University, 33–45.

Reddy, V. 2007. Getting back to the rough ground: Deception and 'social living', in *Social Intelligence: From Brian to Culture,* edited by N. Emery et al. Oxford: Oxford University Press, 219–44.

Senge, P.M. 1999. *The Fifth Discipline: The Art & Practice of the Learning Organization*. London: Random House.

Trim, P.R.J. and Lee, Y-I. 2004. Enhancing customer service and organizational learning through qualitative research. *Qualitative Market Research: An International Journal*, 7 (4), 284–92.

Trim, P.R.J. and Lee, Y-I. 2007. Placing organizational learning in the context of strategic management. *Business Strategy Series*, 8 (5), 335–42.

Website

See http://www.guardian.co.uk/uk/2009/feb/02/snow-london-travel-chaos [accessed: 29 November 2010].

9

Devising an Effective Counter Threat Strategy

9.0   Introduction

Managers in organizations that have been affected by a cyber attack do not always want to talk about what happened and how people in the organization responded to the attack. This suggests that there may be concern within the organization regarding how the public will view management's ability and this may have a knock-on effect vis-à-vis the share value of the organization. It can also be suggested that those that launch a successful cyber attack gain publicity and in so doing stimulate other like-minded individuals/groups to use the same vulnerability. What has started to emerge is that senior managers are becoming increasingly concerned about the range and intensity of attacks and about the role played by the board of directors. For example, a lack of transparency is sometimes linked with a dysfunctional management system and an organizational value system that is underpinned by a blame culture. It can also be argued that senior management need to put in place a transformational management process in order for a collectivist decision-making process to emerge and to activate strategic change (Lee 2009). What needs to be realized by senior managers today is that there is every chance that an attack of some kind (it could be a sustained attack) will be unleashed on the organization they work for and that a flexible and realistic risk mitigation strategy needs to be in place to repulse an attack and at the same time ensure that the organization's image does not suffer in any way.

The chapter starts with an explanation of why managers need to put in place an effective counterintelligence policy (Section 9.1) and then goes on to outline how senior managers can devise an organizational cyber security policy (Section 9.2). Next appears the importance of training (Section 9.3), which is then followed by a conclusion (Section 9.4).

9.1   An Effective Counterintelligence Policy

Senior management can think in terms of establishing a counterintelligence operation so that security is viewed as a core activity, but this will only be the case where the organization has the resources to do this. A high percentage of companies do not have the skills or the resources to be able to make security a core activity; however, a possible alternative approach would be to hire the services of an external security software company to do this for them. There are highly sophisticated security systems and tools in the market and these can be reinforced with advice and consultancy services. A formal counterintelligence policy can have the objective of ensuring that in-house security staff, as well as strategists, are involved in a formal and structured counterintelligence operation. Together with external experts, they can undertake specific security related topics and provide insights into possible future cyber attacks and their expected consequences. Managers can use this intelligence to devise risk mitigation strategies and to engage in information sharing, all of which is aimed at establishing or reinforcing a security culture. A formal counterintelligence policy will help IT managers to devise realistic budgets and to defend their budgets when questioned by their peers. As well as advocating that the organization needs to upgrade its IT systems and technology, it is also possible that advice will be given to partner organizations so that they can upgrade the organization's computer systems in order to ensure that interoperability is attained. A word of warning is needed here. For example, it is a well-known fact that upgrades can come with unexpected vulnerabilities and it may be better to stay with the old/present system and then run 'early adoption' risks.

It is possible that there will be an informal component or side to the counterintelligence activities, and such activities will draw on information inputs and advice from staff based in trade associations, professional organizations, as well as partner organizations (suppliers, wholesalers, retailers, and strategic alliance members for example). Managers based in organizations that have been attacked will need to share information with a range of stakeholders and raise industry standards by promoting best practice associated with defending against cyber attacks. The UK's Centre for the Protection of National Infrastructure (CPNI) and the Information Exchange initiative has this as a main objective. Industry specialists seem to suggest that even if those responsible for safeguarding the organization are well trained and have a high skill level, the type and variety of attacks on an organization are well beyond what a typical organization can defend against. The level of competence of those carrying out cyber attacks is likely to increase through time. As a result, this will test the organization's level of resilience and management's ingenuity to predict and defend against future threats. It is for these reasons that a robust and flexible counterintelligence policy needs to be put in place. By being committed to effective computer security and a high level of information assurance, an adequate risk assessment policy will be adopted and a formal risk mitigation strategy will be devised and implemented. This should also have the effect of management adopting a holistic view of what risk entails and being better informed about which parts of the business are at risk. For example, a cyber attack on an organization that results in money being transferred out of the company to an illegal entity, will result in legal costs as action is taken to recover the money stolen; and it will have implications in the sense that additional money may need to be borrowed from a bank to cover the immediate loss. Furthermore, there are opportunity costs involved such as the loss of production (production lines may need to be closed down and people laid off work) and legal action may be taken against the organization itself by suppliers that have not been paid owing to the fact that the money is not available to pay them. A well-formulated counterintelligence policy and strategy, which are outlined in the organization's business continuity policy, will take into account all business activities and transactions throughout the supply chain and extend into the marketing channels (wholesalers and retailers). Hence it is necessary for staff to engage in communication with stakeholders that fulfils a number of internal marketing objectives (keeping people throughout the partnership arrangement informed about what security arrangements are in place and which additional security arrangements are to be put in place). This should result in partner organizations investing in higher levels of security and as a result of enhanced security, the organization's supply chain should be less vulnerable as the separate business activities are monitored more closely and encased in a strategic management decision-making process. In other words, senior managers need to ensure that those that deal with suppliers on a day-to-day or week-to-week basis think through the security objectives and priorities, and refine and redefine matters so that their expectations of what the supplier(s) can and does deliver are met.

It has to be acknowledged that IT managers are not always aware of and have experience of the various cyber attacks orchestrated by young adults. Those that are intent on penetrating and disrupting an organization's databases and information systems, can be thought of as young or reasonably young and irresponsible, and are most likely to share their successes and adventures with their peers or similar individuals or groups of individuals. Those that are intent on stealing data or sabotaging an organization's data base(s) are known to be hardened individuals who are normally members of criminal gangs and syndicates. Although it is important to acknowledge that acts of hacking and fraud are carried out by a range of people, from various socio-economic groups and typically from a wide age range, international criminal syndicates are often located in geographical areas where they cannot be traced or where they have set up bases that can be closed down and moved at speed. International criminal syndicates operate outside the reach of law enforcement agencies and are motivated by profit, and are self-sustaining. To this one can add highly gifted and disillusioned staff who are out to take revenge on the organization that they have worked for and which they feel has let them down in some way. In this case, they are more likely to steal data and information and sell it or distribute it to third parties for wider and possibly free dissemination. It also can be noted that sometimes disillusioned staff work in unison with overseas government representatives or staff employed by front companies operated by overseas governments that are seeking to acquire data and information through illegal means. There are markets emerging for stolen data and information, and in some parts of the world, there are specialist organizations stealing data to order, which appear to be operating as 'normal' business models.

Often, internally orchestrated attacks are carried out for financial gain and it is becoming increasingly apparent that a variety of direct and indirect means are being used to identify human resource vulnerabilities that can be targeted and manipulated. Both education (interpreted as staff development) and training (skill enhancement) are critically important to make staff aware of what threats exist and how these threats can be repulsed and eradicated. Staff development and training programmes are ongoing and can be used to educate employees with respect to current and evolving cyber security risks. Governments around the world are providing advice on what needs to be done to make organizations more resilient and how industry can co-ordinate their resilience efforts. Although government can provide advice and support, through their intelligence and security agencies, and provide the necessary leadership to ensure that industry works in a joint manner (the sharing of information and the lobbying of government for greater regulation) to reduce both cyber and physical threats on companies in the industry, managers need to be aware that even if they identify and quantify all the potential cyber attacks they may not be able to guard against low probability, high impact events that produce real problems for the organization. It has to be understood that it is not possible for senior management to eliminate all potential threats by putting in place a comprehensive counterintelligence strategy, but what needs to be done is for management to prioritize risks and mitigate the risks accordingly.

It is important at this juncture to reflect on what the difference is between security and counterintelligence. Security can be widely interpreted but is in essence concerned with training and putting in place proper technical measures to repel a range of cyber and non-cyber attacks. Counterintelligence is proactive and is concerned with identifying (through a means of covert and overt legally conducted operations) potential cyber attacks that may be unleashed on an organization. Indeed, the following example outlines clearly why senior management in organizations operating in a sensitive industry need to implement a counterintelligence policy and strategy (West 2011: 2):

> *HACKERS have penetrated the security networks of the world's biggest defence company, Lockheed Martin, sparking fears that other groups' systems may have been breached.*
>
> *The intruders are thought to have created duplicates to electronic keys made by American technology group, EMC Corporation. Its security division, RSA, was hit by a sophisticated attack in March.*
>
> *RSA's electronic keys enable company employees to log into their computer network securely when they are out of the office. Its technology is used by most Fortune 500 companies and federal agencies in America. The website also cites case studies from Rolls-Royce and Bentley cars, Staffordshire police, the French ministry of education, Virgin Blue, the airline, and the Bedfordshire and Luton fire and rescue service.*
>
> *Lockheed produces some of the most advanced military hardware in the world, including the F-35 Joint Strike Fighter, F-22 Raptor and is a significant contractor on America's nuclear weapons programme.*
>
> *Reports suggest Lockheed has temporarily disabled remote access and sent 90,000 replacement keys to staff. Employees were also told to rest all passwords as a precaution.*
>
> *Sources said military contractors typically do not keep classified data on computers that can be accessed remotely. Other defence groups use the keys – sold under the SecurID brand – and the Pentagon confirmed it also uses a limited number.*
>
> *Raytheon, a top-five US defence group, said it took immediate company-wide action when the RSA breach emerged. It said: 'As a result of these actions, we prevented a widespread disruption of our network'.*

In the years ahead, it is likely that more attention will be given to monitoring networks and developing network systems that contain highly sophisticated sensors that report and obstruct and eradicate unlawful intrusions. This is being done already, for example, Cisco operate the Monitoring, Analysis, and Response System (MARS) that (see http://www.cisco.com/en/US/products/ps6241/index.html [accessed: 3 December 2010]): identifies threats on the Cisco network by an integrated process of '"learning" the topology, configuration, and behaviour' of the environment and 'making precise recommendations for threat mitigation, including the ability to visualize the attack path and identify the source of the threat; simplifying incident management and response through integration with Cisco Security Manager security management software'.

Faulty systems need to be identified quickly and action taken to close them down or eradicate the fault. If a fault in a system is not rectified early on it may produce a major malfunction, which then causes the system to collapse or gives rise to an explosion or a major failure that has a cascading effect. Being able to isolate a failure before it affects other systems is crucial because dealing in real time saves time and money. However, it has to be borne in mind that when an electricity generating station fails or a series of relay stations fail, those controlling the supply of power do not have time to intervene because the occurrence happens far too quickly and there could be further cascading effects that increase the intensity of the problem and stop a back-up system from operating. In order to stop a system failing completely or knocking out another power generating system, it may be useful to shut the system down.

It could be, for example, that an independent security company is hired to monitor the activities of an activist group that is known to be targeting companies in a specific industry. The security company may ask its staff to participate in online discussion groups and cyber conferences in order to gain intelligence relating to possible future cyber attacks, as this would allow companies in the industry to put security systems in place and to have public relations personnel briefed in the event that adverse publicity results. Normally, certain contingencies would be in place that allowed only specified company individuals to act as spokesperson for the organization in the event of an incident/major event. The logic of this is that only approved material would be made available/communicated to a wider public owing to the fact that contradictory statements may cause adverse publicity and ultimately affect the company's share value for example. Having the appropriate personnel briefed is extremely important in the case of an attack because social websites in particular are emerging as places where information is communicated and exchanged, and these will, it is argued, become increasingly important as less reliance is placed on newspaper articles by certain age groups in society. Although there are many ethical issues associated with intelligence gathering, it can be argued that a number of large corporations have, for some time now, been employing personnel that worked previously for government intelligence agencies to head up their competitive intelligence units (Prescott and Miller 2001). One conclusion that can be drawn is that investing adequately in cyber counterintelligence that produces meaningful results is likely to be a big commitment and one that is going to have to be maintained and strengthened through time.

9.2   Devising an Organizational Cyber Security Policy

There will be security gaps, but what senior management can do is prioritize identifiable risks and share best practice throughout the industry. Organizational heads of security can think in terms of building adequate defences against cyber attacks, and this will mean liaising with government, which can provide both technical assistance and clearly defined advisory support. Reflecting on organizational sustainability, it is necessary for senior managers to put in place a cyber security policy, which incorporates or commits the organization to embrace training as a means of constantly updating the skill base of the organization and in effect making sure that a cyber attack will be repulsed. The main objective of the cyber security policy would be to require senior managers to look beyond their day-to-day business environment and to think about the wider issues and threats most likely to confront the business over the short-, middle- and long-term.

One factor that policy advisors need to take into account is that the private sector owns an increasing percentage of the nation's critical information infrastructure and that they have responsibility for maintaining it and defending it against attack, both physical and cyber. This introduces levels of responsibility that formerly were often limited to governments. So the key question emerges: do private sector staff possess the necessary skills to counter a wide range of hacking, cracking and industrial espionage orchestrated attacks? The Cyber Security Challenge UK, officially launched by The Rt Hon Baroness Neville-Jones, Minister for Security at University College London on 26 July 2010, has as its objective, to identify talented individuals who can defend the UK against cyber attacks of various types and who wish to embark on a career in cyber security (CAMIS Newsletter 2010: 4) (see www.cybersecuritychallenge.org.uk [accessed: July 2010]).

Another question can be posed: how are specialists from the private sector going to liaise with government specialists in order that a complete range of cyber security skills are developed that act as appropriate countermeasures across industry sectors? Government technologists are looking at the issues and are focusing on the types of technologies that are being deployed to penetrate or disrupt networks. Government experts are looking at what type of documentation needs to be produced to enable those acquiring cyber skills to update themselves and be viewed as well able to repulse an attack. Bearing in mind the above, it can be argued that organizations in both the private and the public sectors will in the years ahead need to focus more on acquiring a diverse range of cyber security skills, and that personnel from both sectors will at times need to work together in order to raise the security skill base of employees and those more generally in the industry in which the organization competes. At the same time, they will need to invest in higher levels of security, which may include testing the systems and networks in place more frequently for their robustness. As regards the latter, more use can be made of internal/external 'white hat' penetration testers and this is likely to be the case.

Attacks on financial institutions and banks in particular are likely to increase as the cost of cyber attacks comes down. A relatively small investment, within the reach of even small criminal groups, can buy viable attack software and hire botnets or other facilities needed to run them. The Mariposa malware that was unleashed did not represent an attack on banks as such – it attacked individuals and stole their passwords and other details. It can be argued that the security software in place at banks would not have been able to detect such an attack. Larry Barrett's report (3 March 2010) on the incident has been produced herewith (see http://www.internetnews.com/security/article.php/3868446/Mariposa-Hackers-Busted-in-Giant-Botnet-Scam.htm [accessed: 3 December 2010]):

> Security software firms working with international law enforcement agencies, the FBI and the Georgia Tech Information Security Center teamed up to neutralize and eventually arrest three Spanish men who allegedly masterminded a massive botnet scam that ensnared more than 13 million PCs.
>
> Three men, who called themselves the 'Nightmare Days Team' and dubbed their botnet projects 'Mariposa', were arrested at their Basque Country residence by Spanish authorities last month after a year-long investigation by local law enforcement agencies and security software

vendors Panda Security, which is headquartered in Bilbao, Spain, and Defence Intelligence of Ottawa, Ontario, Canada.

Though security experts described the hacking trio as 'relatively unskilled cyber criminals', they managed to use Mariposa – the Spanish word for butterfly – to steal account log-in information for social media sites, online e-mail services, user names and passwords to banking accounts and credit card data by infiltrating more than 12.7 million compromised personal, corporate and government IP addresses in more than 190 countries.

Officials said the botnet was shutdown on Dec. 23, 2009 after operating largely unhindered for almost a year. Mariposa accessed more than 13 million PCs, making it one of the <u>largest and most destructive botnets</u> in history.

'Our preliminary analysis indicates that the botmasters did not have advanced hacking skills', Pedro Bustamante, Panda Security's senior research advisor, said in a <u>blog posting</u> detailing the attacks and subsequent investigation.

9.3   The Importance of Training

It is evident from this example that training needs to go in tandem with a cyber security awareness programme so that people are up-to-date with respect to identifying or knowing how to assess the vulnerability of a computer system, and where and from whom assistance can be received in order to rectify the problem should one occur. The fact that the banking sector and the energy sector are at risk from cyber attack, is of growing concern to community leaders owing to the fact that disruption and disorder can be inflicted on a widely dispersed population, with the most vulnerable members of society being at most risk. Areas potentially at risk are: services and the supply of water and electricity. Another possible area of attack is food and retailing, owing to the fact that these are necessary industries and there is a high level of interdependence in the supply chain. High levels of interdependence requires that managers, if they want to ensure that their organization is able to provide continuity of supply, invest time and money in devising workable security systems that are underpinned by adequate management control systems. Systems which affect the whole community need valid security, and once a security procedure is in place it has to be maintained.

Individual managers might well ask the question: what are the rewards for ensuring that an adequate cyber security system is in place? In a properly structured company, these rewards should come in terms of organizational benefits and career development. In the case of the latter, individuals need support and resources to develop to their full potential. This again raises the issue of managers thinking seriously about the benefits associated with formal cyber security training programmes and staff development programmes, and thinking in terms of how organizational learning can be embraced more fully. Attention is also needed with respect to which learning style(s) is appropriate for ensuring that the organization's value system is enriched through time. An integrated learning approach, which has at its heart a clearly defined set of learning aims and objectives, will require that managers and their staff embrace the concept of risk more fully and think about managing risk in an appropriate manner. Risk is organization-specific, but organizations are interlinked with other industries and with national well-being. For example, London is a world financial hub and over exposure by the banks in certain markets can and does cause concern for the UK regulators and their political masters. Should the UK lose a component of the banking industry for whatever reason, then it is more than likely that the UK economy will suffer (loss of jobs and also alterative competitive bases being established in other countries).

Industrial espionage has been an issue for hundreds of years, and is likely to continue as nations compete ever harder to gain a sustainable competitive advantage for their domestic industries. Cyber attacks represent another way for those so willed to conduct an espionage programme. Organizations that lack controls and reporting mechanisms are likely to be at risk from insider and externally orchestrated attacks (especially internal fraud for example).

It is axiomatic that it is not possible for senior management to put in place 100 per cent protection of the organization's assets. But this is no reason for not trying. Organizations can and should try to match 'best practice' in these areas. Those that do not, stand out, and attract attacks.

Training teams requires an understanding of the benefits associated with experiential learning, which in turn can help management to produce a learning organization. A good starting point is for senior management to put in place a separate monitoring unit or appoint a member of staff to log the number and type of cyber attacks carried out on organizations in their industry, and then to establish how the nature of these attacks change or are likely to change. For example, if managers in large organizations make it more difficult for threat agents to penetrate an organization and steal data or money then organized criminals may well focus their attention elsewhere. Hot desking has been taken a stage further and many employees now work remotely, e.g., from their own home. This raises a whole set of security issues and an organization that embarks down this route has possibly weighed up the economic costs associated with maintaining a small office based group of staff with the threats posed.

There are a number of countermeasures that can be used to curtail intrusions and provide more robust security. For example, Lopez and Resendez (2009: 371) have made reference to the use of firewalls, intrusion detection systems and methods of encryption to defend networks against attack. Tools are available for researching network attacks and Lopez and Resendez (2009: 373) have outlined the usefulness of Honeypots, which they defined as: 'false information servers that are strategically placed in a network, which are set up with false information disguised as files of important nature'. It is acknowledged that Honeypots are highly specialized and because of this, there is no reason to expect that the average sized business will deploy them. Most likely, they will rely on expert security measures.

Lopez and Resendez (2009: 373), drawing on the work of Spitzner, explain that a group of Honeypots are known as a Honeynet, for example:

> *Honeynets are a tool that integrates different types of Honetpots into a single network, providing a wide group of possible threats that has two purposes: to give a rogue user a wider 'menu' of options to perform different exploits and to give systems administrators more information for study. It makes the attack more appealing for the rogue user due to the fact that Honeypots can increase the possibilities, targets, exploits.*

Cyber-forensics is an area that needs attention and organizations need to put resources into developing in-house expertise and/or engage specialists that can use various forensics in order to analyse and interpret computer-based records. Cyber-forensics is expected to accelerate in importance as it provides a means for senior managers and law enforcement officers to establish, sooner rather than later, exactly what damage was caused by an attacker having entered organization's computer network and computer system.

At this point it is useful to reflect on what is meant by the term Information Assurance (IA). Singh et al. (2009: 294) suggest that:

Information assurance is often used interchangeably with information security. But in specific terms, information assurance can be defined as information operations that protect and defend information and information systems by ensuring their availability, integrity, authentication, confidentiality, and non-repudiation.

CESG have provided a useful definition of what Information Assurance (IA) represents (see http://www.cesg.gov.uk/about_us/whatisia.shtml [accessed: 3 December 2010]):

Information Assurance is the confidence that information systems will protect the information they handle and will function as they need to, when they need to, under the control of legitimate users.

There is little information that exists that will not at one time or another be stored or transmitted electronically.

Information on paper as soon as it is fixed or input into a computer, enters the electronic world. From here the information can be changed, deleted or broadcast to the world. Electronic information must be readily available when needed and trusted to be accurate. Sometimes there are confidentiality concerns. Ensuring the confidentiality, availability and integrity of all electronically held information is the goal. 'Information Assurance' is the term we use to describe this goal.

Through the use of appropriate security products and procedures we hope to achieve reasonable assurance that electronic information is adequately protected from unauthorised change or dissemination and ensure the information is always available. Helping the owners of electronic information to determine the products and procedures to achieve Information Assurance is what CESG is here for.

An issue which is high up on the agenda of policy makers and their advisors, is the quality of human resources available to deal with failures in critical national infrastructure and most importantly, the availability of fully trained staff and semi or inexperienced staff to deal with failures, disruptions and other important issues relating to continuity of supply and operations. For example, Jones et al. (2009: 278) have made reference to the fact that absenteeism can be a problem and that during periods of absenteeism, less skilled/experienced workers are more likely to cause errors when carrying out work and they have cited issues such as slower repair work and the problems caused by components that fail. Important considerations are the overloading of skilled workers, inadequate management of projects involving a high level of reconfiguring, and having the right equipment and tooling on site within a specified time period.

When writing about training and practice in relation to Computer Network Operations (CNO), Bekatoros et al. (2009: 214) have some useful advice:

> *Myriad organizational changes fail to meet objectives, because people are not given adequate training and practice to perform well in different organizational conditions. It is one thing to tell people that they will be organized differently, that they will have new and fewer, less-formalized job titles, and they will need to adhere to stricter centralization requirements than before; it is another for the people in an organization to adjust to such changes. They need to be trained, and they need to practice. Clearly trial-and-error, on-the-job 'training' will provide much of the training and practice necessary, but this approach is both time-consuming and error-prone. Management should seek out professional help with training and practice, and institute fallback procedures for responding to attacks that exceed the CND [Computer Network Defence] organization's capabilities while in transition.*

Reflecting on the above, it is useful to take into account the thoughts of Caballero (2009: 6–7):

> *Threats are exploited with a variety of attacks, some technical, others not so much. Organizations that focus on the technical attacks and neglect items such as policies and procedures or employee training and awareness are setting up information security for failure ... Most threats today are a mixed blend of automated information gathering, social engineering, and combined exploits, giving the perpetrator endless vectors through which to gain access. Examples of attacks vary from a highly technical remote exploit over the Internet, social-engineering an administrative assistant to reset his password, or simply walking right through an unprotected door in the back of your building.*

9.4   Conclusion

There can be no doubt that companies that have not invested in the latest forms of cyber security will be open to all sorts of attack. Furthermore, developing the required mindset to deal with a variety of threats is paramount and is unlikely to be achieved overnight. It can also be added that as well as technical solutions, human solutions need to be found as threats can manifest from insiders as well as from individuals based outside the organization. Senior managers need to be aware of how an effective cyber security policy can be devised and sold within the organization and also to staff based in partner organizations. It can also be argued that senior managers need to look beyond their own knowledge and expertise, and think in terms of developing a good understanding of what cyber security involves. Owing to the fact that there is great interdependence in the supply chain, it can be argued that potential attackers will identify and target weak links in the business chain and share what information they have found with those of a similar criminal intent. This raises the risk factor and means that senior managers cannot become complacent about security controls and measures, and need to adopt a proactive approach to security. One way in which this can be done is through ensuring that various levels of cyber training are devised for all types of company personnel. The advantage of this is that it would help establish a security culture within the organization, and this should ensure that danger signals are picked up before the threat becomes real, which may have devastating results on the organization and result in it going out of business.

References

Bekatoros, N., Koons, J.L. and Nissen, M.E. 2009. Diagnosing misfits, inducing requirements, and delineating transformations within computer network operations organizations, in *Cyber Security and Global Information Assurance: Threat Analysis and Response Solutions*, edited by K.J. Knapp. Hershey, NY: Information Science Reference, 201–18.

Caballero, A. 2009. Information security essentials for IT managers: Protecting mission-critical systems, in *Managing Information Security*, edited by J.A. Vacca. Burlington, MA: Elsevier, 1–46.

CAMIS Newsletter. 2010. *Cyber Security Challenge UK*, 6 (3), 4.

Jones, D.A., Nozick, L.K., Turnquist, M.A. and Sawaya, W.J. 2009. Pandemic influenza, worker absenteeism and impacts on critical infrastructures, in *Cyber Security and Global Information Assurance: Threat Analysis and Response Solutions*, edited by K.J. Knapp. Hershey, NY: Information Science Reference, 265–82.

Lee, Y-I. 2009. Strategic transformational management in the context of inter-organizational and intra-organizational partnership development, in

Strategizing Resilience and Reducing Vulnerability, edited by P.R.J. Trim and J. Caravelli. New York, NY: Nova Science Publishers, Inc., 181–96.

Lopez, M.J.H.Y. and Resendez, C.F.L. 2009. Introduction, classification and implementation of honeypots, in *Cyber Security and Global Information Assurance: Threat Analysis and Response Solutions*, edited by K.J. Knapp. Hershey, NY: Information Science Reference, 371–82.

Prescott, J.E., and Miller, S.H. (eds). 2001. *Proven Strategies in Competitive Intelligence: Lessons from the Trenches*. Chichester/New York, NY: John Wiley & Sons, Inc.

Singh, P., Singh, P., Park, I., Lee, J. and Rao, H.R. 2009. Information sharing: A survey of information attributes and their relative significance during catastrophic events, in *Cyber Security and Global Information Assurance: Threat Analysis and Response Solutions*, edited by K.J. Knapp. Hershey, NY: Information Science Reference, 283–305.

West, K. 2011. Hackers beat Lockheed defences. *The Sunday Times*. Section 3: Business, 29 May, 2.

Websites

See www.cybersecuritychallenge.org.uk [accessed: July 2010].

See http://www.internetnews.com/security/article.php/3868446/Mariposa-Hackers-Busted-in-Giant-Botnet-Scam.htm [accessed: 3 December 2010].

See http://www.cisco.com/en/US/products/ps6241/index.html [accessed: 3 December 2010].

See http://www.cesg.gov.uk/about_us/whatisia.shtml [accessed: 3 December 2010].

Index

Printed and bound by CPI Group (UK) Ltd, Croydon, CR0 4YY

21/10/2024

01777095-0004